HORIZON

MAY, 1962   ·   VOLUME IV, NUMBER 5

Horizon
A Magazine of the Arts

MAY, 1962 · *VOLUME IV, NUMBER 5*

PUBLISHER
James Parton

EDITORIAL DIRECTOR
Joseph J. Thorndike, Jr.

EDITOR
William Harlan Hale

MANAGING EDITOR
Eric Larrabee

ASSOCIATE EDITOR
Ralph Backlund

ASSISTANT EDITORS
Ada Pesin
Jane Wilson
Albert Bermel

CONTRIBUTING EDITOR
Margery Darrell

EDITORIAL ASSISTANTS
Shirley Abbott, Caroline Backlund
Wendy Buehr, Charles L. Mee, Jr.

COPY EDITOR
Mary Ann Pfeiffer
Assistants: Joan Rehe, Ruth H. Wolfe

ART DIRECTOR
Irwin Glusker
Associate Art Director: Elton Robinson

ADVISORY BOARD
Gilbert Highet, *Chairman*
Frederick Burkhardt   Oliver Jensen
Marshall B. Davidson   Jotham Johnson
Richard M. Ketchum   John Walker

EUROPEAN CONSULTING EDITOR
J. H. Plumb
Christ's College, Cambridge

EUROPEAN BUREAU
Gertrudis Feliu, *Chief*
28 Quai du Louvre, Paris

HORIZON is published every two months by American Heritage Publishing Co., Inc. Executive and editorial offices: 551 Fifth Ave., New York 17, N.Y. HORIZON welcomes contributions but can assume no responsibility for unsolicited material.

All correspondence about subscriptions should be addressed to: HORIZON Subscription Office, 379 West Center St., Marion, Ohio.

Single Copies: $4.50
Annual Subscriptions: $21.00 in the U.S. & Can.
$22.00 elsewhere

An annual index is published every September, priced at $1. HORIZON is also indexed in the *Readers Guide to Periodical Literature.*

Title registered U.S. Patent Office
Second-class postage paid at New York, N.Y.

COVER: The jockey with his invincibly English face is a detail from a larger canvas by George Stubbs (1724–1806), who is so well known for his portraits of horses as to obscure the fact that he painted their owners and handlers with equal directness, honesty, and lack of sentimentality. He was, in fact, one of the best English painters of his time; and as such he was inevitably drawn into the orbit of the Royal Academy of Arts— although more as a satellite than as one of its great, wheeling planets like Reynolds, Gainsborough, or Lawrence. An account of the founding of the R.A. and its once formidable role in English art, as well as its current decline, begins on page 56 and includes a portfolio in gravure of paintings by the artists mentioned above. This detail from *Antinous with his Jockey and Trainer* is reproduced by courtesy of the Duke of Grafton, for whose family Stubbs painted it about 1764.

FRONTISPIECE: Although it has the flat, sinuous look of a Modigliani portrait, this figure of a nude youth is actually some fifteen hundred years old. It is a fragment of Coptic glass intarsia found at Antinoë, in central Egypt, where it probably decorated the walls of a mortuary chapel. The Copts were Christianized native Egyptians; intarsia is a form of inlay using shaped pieces rather than rectangular ones as in mosaic; and Antinoë was a Graeco-Roman colony founded by the emperor Hadrian and named after his favorite Antinoüs (as was, presumably, the horse in Stubbs's painting described above). This fragment is now in the State Collection of Egyptian Art in Munich.

THE WORLDS OF
Robert Sherwood

From school to stage and world stage, he moved through three

eras and spoke memorably for each at his fondest place, his school

Three times in the span of four decades, the late Robert Sherwood stood up at the same place—the campus of Milton Academy outside Boston—to address young Americans: first in prewar 1914, when he was a graduating student himself; then in 1940, as a famous playwright burdened with the onset of new war; then again in 1954, as a hard-tested public figure facing the challenges of a still newer war—the cold one. Around these three appearances, each symptomatic of its time and poignant in its utterance, the critic John Mason Brown builds a portrait that will form the Prologue of the biography of Sherwood on which he is presently working.

June 13, 1914

That Saturday morning in the crowded schoolroom at Milton Academy, ten miles from the heart of Boston, Robert Sherwood at eighteen was already sitting on those tenterhooks which he was to describe years later as "the upholstery of the anxious seat." Outside, the June sun brightened the green of the school's wide lawns and the red bricks and white columns of its Georgian buildings, and created the illusion of that calm which is supposed to be academic.

This was an illusion to which young Sherwood did not at the moment surrender. He was a gawky, squab-chested giant, more bone than flesh, whose body within the past two years had stretched another unneeded two inches until it rested, towering uneasily at six-feet-seven. As one of the seventeen members of the graduating class, he was unnaturally clean for the occasion and wore the uniform of the day —white flannels, a dark blue coat and vest, a school tie of orange and blue stripes, and the kind of choking high stiff collar in which Herbert Hoover would have found comfort. He was one of two classmates whose hair was jauntily parted in the middle, a fashion which was to be the hallmark of a generation of American males. His lantern face, young and assured as it was, however, knew no jauntiness, and his stomach no June warmth.

He was a little pale, a little nervous, and with reason. Not because scarlet fever, then a common menace, had bedded several of his classmates in the shining new infirmary. Nor because he and his parents had been informed that, as a result of his sustained gift for gathering appallingly bad marks, he would not receive a diploma for work done well but a certificate for having been physically present. This was bad news, though stale. He and his family had lived with it for two unhappy weeks.

The reason for young Sherwood's disquiet was the copy of the "Programme for Commencement" which he held in his hands. It was a disturbing reminder (as if he needed one) of what lay inexorably ahead. The first three of the items it listed were a hymn, a prayer, and the award of

prizes; the last three, the award of diplomas by the President of the Board of Trustees, an address by Harvard's Professor Bliss Perry, and the school song. Sandwiched in the middle of these traditional features was the announcement that read, "Valedictory: Robert Emmet Sherwood," an honor, by the way, conferred on him by the vote of his classmates. The announcement was tucked in the middle of the program even as tucked in the inner pocket of Sherwood's dark blue coat was his script. Tucked as surely within his heart was the lack of ease of the speaker who has not yet been called on.

When his turn came, he extricated himself from his chair, unfurled his body, walked to the lectern, spread his manuscript, waited for the applause to end, and then began to read, having to stoop to the podium like a feeding crane to bring his pages into focus.

What did he say to this audience of three hundred, composed of parents and families who had driven out in carriages or Stanley Steamers and Model-T Fords, and of boys, new and old, the squeaky and squirming small fry as well as his frog-throated and attentive classmates? What did he say at this school in which the recurrent names were Saltonstall, Forbes, Wolcott, Hallowell, Pierce, Robbins, Wigglesworth, and Sherwood? What do all valedictorians say, at least in part even now, in schools public and private, up and down the country, almost by obligation, when the hour of liberation is at last at hand and the voice of the boy orator is heard in the land?

To his credit Sherwood did not exhume, "And this above all, to thine own self be true," as if he had heard the first Polonius speaking it for the first time. Yet in his own way, rediscovering the old truths as the young will and making them their own by the sincerity of their wonder, he pulled out the unvarying stops of nostalgia, responsibility, and trust. He spoke, as doubtless thousands of his contemporaries were speaking from thousands of platforms that early June, at a time when the skies above them appeared to be almost cloudless, when their futures were theirs to make as they chose, when oceans were still oceans, when foreign affairs were foreign indeed, and America the beautiful still seemed smiling and secure.

He spoke from within the walls of his years, his school, his experiences there, his emotions at parting, his expectations, and a universal confidence. He thanked his teachers. He thanked his school because Milton, in spite of his grades and his mountain of black marks, had meant much to him and was always to hold a special place in his heart.

There were Sherwood touches in the valedictorian's ever-recurrent themes—schoolboy sproutings of his humor and foretastes of his fluent clarity and mixed realism and idealism. He spoke of escape. Escape into what? Of course, into "that unknown which lies beyond and into which we are about to pass," a world vaguely felt to be "a marvelous place" where "the perfect freedom may be found."

By JOHN MASON BROWN

He then appraised his own class, apologizing for its lack of distinction in scholarship and athletics. "Are we not, after all," he asked, "a commonplace lot, not to be remembered with any more interest or respect than is held for every class which graduates from this school?" In the future lay atonement. "There will come a time—it seems a long way off," said he, "when we shall be old men returning on Graduates' Day. . . . We are determined that we shall then bring some offering of attainment to increase the good name of the school."

He was climbing to his peroration, as planes and speakers will for altitude. His was the pious valedictory hope that it would be ultimately said of his class "when we pass through the gates for the very last time" that "we of the class of 1914" had indeed, in terms of the school motto, dared to be true.

He was through. The ordeal was over. The "Programme" continued to its close, after which luncheon (cold salmon and potato salad, no doubt) was served at Robbins House. His masters, his classmates and their parents, said their good-byes and dispersed. They clucked to their horses, or cranked their cars, leaving this Norman Rockwell scene in its Sargent setting, many of them soon to sail for what they expected to be a carefree summer in Europe.

Sherwood within a few days headed for the State of Washington to visit his eldest brother, Arthur. They were all in a vacation mood. A new world was at hand, but it was not to be the world that he and his contemporaries took for granted. Two weeks later, in distant Sarajevo, a student assassinated the Austrian Archduke Ferdinand and his Duchess, with results that were to involve America in ways that could not be foreseen. A prophecy for a class had been turned into a farewell to an age.

A June 14, 1940

Another commencement, again at Milton. Sherwood faced his audience this time as an aroused individual, passionately committed. He was a man very much in the news and the news was very much in him. Two and a half months before, his *There Shall Be No Night* had opened in New York, making it clear that the fate of Finland had forced Sherwood, like his peace-loving scientist in that play, Dr. Valkonen, to reach the agonized decision in a world imperiled by Nazi, Fascist, and Soviet forces that the time comes when "there is only one form of work that matters—resistance—blind, dogged, desperate resistance."

The previous month Sherwood had made his position even clearer by joining William Allen White on the Committee to Defend America by Aiding the Allies. Only four days before he came to speak at Milton the full-page "STOP HITLER NOW" advertisement, which he had written for that Committee and for the publication of which he and some friends paid, had created a sensation when it was run in newspapers across the country. By bluntly asserting that "anyone who argues that the Nazis will considerately wait until we are ready to go to war is either an imbecile or a traitor," it had infuriated those living on the sedatives of impossible hopes, but at a White House press conference it won the public endorsement of President Roosevelt, whom Sherwood then did not know. Dr. Joseph Goebbels' response from Berlin was acid in its realism. "Stop Hitler? With what?" he had sneeringly asked.

This time nine hundred people, including thirty-three students from war-torn countries overseas, were in the Robert Saltonstall gymnasium that had been built since Sherwood had spoken as valedictorian, and expectancy was as crisp in the June warmth as the bite of frost in winter. When the audience was gathering, a graduate said to a master, "I'll bet Bob Sherwood will launch out and outdo himself today because of what has been on the air." What had been on the radio, what had turned the day's headlines into mourning bands, what was on the minds of everyone, was the news that Paris had fallen to Hitler. With France conquered by the Nazis, it appeared inevitable that England's turn would come next and that she would be conquered quickly.

Sherwood had seen the papers the night before as he took the midnight train to Boston, and the news of the fall of Paris had seemed to him "to mark this as the blackest day in all history." He could not sleep. He did not want to. He was racingly awake. After such a catastrophe he knew that he neither would nor could deliver the next morning the traditional commencement address he had prepared. Accordingly, he tore it up and sat up all night in his compartment trying to write down what he really felt about "the obscure and terrible future."

At forty-four Sherwood returned to Milton as an alumnus bringing "an uncommon offering of attainment." He had made his name in journalism as the editor and motion-picture critic of the old *Life*. He was a fabulously successful and ever-deepening playwright who had twice won the Pulitzer Prize for drama. He had prospered in Hollywood as well as on Broadway. He was a past president of the Dramatists Guild, a co-founder of the Playwrights Company, and a member of the National Institute of Arts and Letters. Yet it was not only because of his successes and distinction that he aroused interest as he jackknifed his long body into his chair on the platform. The man mattered more than the playwright that morning; the man at last awake in an America for the most part sleeping; the controversial figure praised by those alerted in his fashion but condemned by isolationists and America Firsters as a pacifist who had become a warmonger.

If tired from his ordeal on the train, Sherwood did not

show it. His tension routed his fatigue. Beneath his shaggy eyebrows the darkness of a darkening world was in his deep brown eyes. His head seemed small, coming as a climax to a body so extended. His broad mouth was thinned by resolution. In spite of the gray in his short-cropped mustache, his hair, no longer parted in the middle but at the right, was a smooth black. He had the look of a youngish man with energies well used and a reservoir of energies untapped. In appearance he was more worldling than aesthete and well-tailored though casual. Totally American as he was, he suggested, until he spoke, a lean, trim, elongated British major in mufti.

Some think they remember that he began haltingly, with pauses that sounded like intermissions. Others recall only the speed with which they were possessed by the intensity of feeling that plainly possessed him. According to one master, his address was "electric in its communicated emotion"; according to another, it was "one of the four or five most moving speeches" he ever heard. Sherwood was conscious of the "ugly responsibility" he faced in having to stand up and talk to a group of boys who were going from a school he cherished into the dreadful world that confronted them. He chose as his theme the threats of that world, and the follies and failures that had brought it into being. He did not pull his punches.

Inevitably, he went back to 1914 to re-create, for the young to whom he spoke, the world of his youth as he had known it eight or nine years before the oldest boy in his audience was born. He confessed that he and his classmates on their Commencement Day had foreseen no complications in the future. They did not watch the skies for bombers, fearing an invasion from the air, because "at that time, it was all an airplane could do to fly as far as from Providence to Boston." They did not listen to alarming news broadcasts because there was no radio, and if there had been, the news would not have been alarming. "In our innocence, and our ignorance, we had virtually nothing to worry about."

He mentioned Sarajevo and the shots there which had started a chain of explosions that had blown this other world to bits. "In the twenty-six years that have passed since then," he added grimly, "all efforts to reassemble that world, or to construct a newer, more reasonable world, have failed tragically. Our world now resembles chaos worse confounded." He referred to his three years at Harvard and his experiences overseas in The Canadian Black Watch in World War I when, wounded, he had been a patient in a long series of hospitals in England and France. "I never wanted to see war again," he admitted, "and I firmly believed that I never should."

Then he turned to the twenties, castigating them for their "disastrous folly" and as "the age of disillusionment, which sowed the seeds of despair which were to grow into the present calamity." Proudly he recalled how the United States had gone into the First War "in the finest spirit." With shame he remembered how we came out of it, cynically announcing that we had fought in vain, that our young men had died for nothing, and that we flatly refused to do our share toward keeping the peace we had helped to win.

He minced no words in attacking "the appalling corruption of the Harding administration . . . the hysterical revelry in paper profits of the Coolidge 'boom' . . . the hypocrisy and crime of Prohibition," and the literature of futility which, Russian in its origins, had grown up in this country and in England, France, and Germany. He told the young they had the right to ask their elders why, instead of a more perfect civilization, there had been such retrogression to savagery and the jungle since 1914. This was the tormenting question he asked himself, too. He was fully aware of the enormous developments in communications, made possible by the automobile, the airplane, radio, and motion pictures; the vast social reforms in the emancipation of women, the strides in collective bargaining, the recognition in all democracies of certain essential human rights; the ambitious experiment in the Soviet Union; the inspiring advance of the medical profession in psychology and the exploration of the infinite mysteries of the human mind; and the heartening, remarkable spread of education in all parts of the earth.

Then came the avowal of the hideous truth which he had faced and which he felt it his duty to call to the attention of the young. When on this June morning Sherwood quoted the words "Dare To Be True"—the George Herbert line on the Milton shield—he did so to remind his hearers that over the portals of Heidelberg University used to be inscribed the beautiful assurance that the institution was dedicated "To the Living Truth," which the Nazis had later changed to read "To the *German* Truth." "You cannot 'Dare To Be True,'" said Sherwood, "in a world ruled by Hitler. You cannot dare to be free, or even to be human. You can only dare to die."

"I'm afraid," he added, "that, as commencement addresses go, this one rates among the gloomiest ever delivered." He asked forgiveness by saying on this historic day "we have learned of the fall of Paris" and "my mind is full of that terrible knowledge." One and only one expression of hope he gave to the graduating class. His own essential faith in the goodness that is in man still survived after these tragic twenty-six years, and he was confident that it would continue to do so as long as he lived. "I hope you will find in your own lives that this faith is justified. I hope you will see a world in which men at last have found a way to live in peace."

In the next weeks Sherwood had letters from two of the mothers who were present that day. They upbraided him for his depressing speech, and in effect asked, "How could you look into those innocent, hopeful faces and say such awful things?" He could only reply to these good ladies that he had been unable to bring himself to tell lies to their sons.

April 28, 1954

It was to honor Milton's graduates who had dared to die for their country that he mounted the platform in the gymnasium this Wednesday night, fourteen years and two wars later. Twenty-three men had given their lives in the First War, two of them his classmates in 1914; forty-four in the Second War, including four of the "innocent" and "hopeful" who had heard him in 1940; and four during the Korean conflict. Seventy-one of the approximately 1,900 enlisted alumni was a small number compared to the more than 557,000 Americans who had died in the three wars, but it was a large number for Milton because Milton was a small school. The tragic aggregate was gallantly represented in the fraction.

Many of the families, friends, and teachers of the dead were crowded in the gymnasium, along with the young, to hear this Alumni War Memorial Foundation lecture. It was the twentieth to be delivered since 1924 on the subject of "The Responsibilities and Opportunities Attached to Leadership in a Democracy." The previous speakers had ranged from former Assistant Secretary of the Navy Franklin D. Roosevelt and Canada's Governor General Vincent Massey, to Boston's Bishop A. Lowell Lawrence, Germany's ex-Chancellor Heinrich Bruening, Britain's John Buchan, and America's Newton D. Baker and General George C. Marshall. Sherwood was the second Miltonian to be asked to speak and, remembering 1914 and 1940, he had written the headmaster, Arthur B. Perry, Bliss Perry's son, "It would seem to be a mistake to invite me, associated as I am with doom." He was associated with much more.

He had earned his place among the eminent. Everyone knew of his involvement with events. Everyone knew that he had worked on Roosevelt's speeches and been his friend; that he had served as Overseas Director of the Office of War Information, and that there were few in high positions in the free world unknown to him. He was a distinguished playwright who had evolved into an acclaimed biographer, a man of the theatre very much at home on the larger stage of affairs. In addition to achieving fame for his talents, he had become famous for his goodness. Because of his prestige, he faced the hazards of being turned into a national institution, the fluent and fearless spokesman of the democratic faith. Every good cause and committee turned to him as a sponsor, and his conscience permitted him to decline few.

His honors had multiplied. He had won two more Pulitzer Prizes, one for drama with *There Shall Be No Night,* the other for biography with *Roosevelt and Hopkins.* In *The Best Years of Our Lives* he had written a film that had collected nine Oscars. He had been elevated from the National Institute of Arts and Letters to the Academy, served as Trustee of Milton and an Overseer at Harvard, and received honorary degrees from Dartmouth, Yale, Harvard,

and Bishop's University. He had grown and grown, but never stodgy. He could be as gay as ever, was as fond of frivolity, and as grateful for laughter. Yet on his face that night was a sadness which tugged at the hearts of perceptive spectators; a weariness, too.

Most people took his height to be the measure of his strength. And uncommonly strong he was, but only with a strength resolute enough to triumph over frequent illness and the torture of having had to live for years with a recurrent and terrible facial nervous disorder, double *tic douloureux,* which had attacked him again only the week before. The pain he had become accustomed to rising above was on his face that evening.

He looked twenty-five, not fourteen, years older as he sat on the platform with the lights stressing the gray streaks in his dark hair, the white plumes of his still scraggly eyebrows, the darkness of his mourning eyes, the whiteness of his crisp mustache, and the strong downward pull of the lines under his lower lids and around his nostrils and mouth. The British major that a Royal Academician could have painted in 1940 had been transformed by the years into an El Greco in a dinner jacket.

Sherwood's day had been exhausting. He had spoken that morning on the political aspects of strategy at the Naval War College in Newport, and speaking remained for him an ordeal. He had guessed he would be nervous at Milton, and he was. To take his mind off his speech, he had asked his old friend, tutor, and favorite master at Milton, Albert W. Hunt, to dine with him at the Ritz-Carlton in Boston. Though they had talked pleasantly of old times, his nervousness grew. It was even greater when they had driven to Milton. There, to subdue it, he took a giant's slug of gin, uncontaminated by ice, ten minutes before he walked onto the platform with the headmaster Mr. Perry.

It was not only conquered pain or the fatigue of a tiring day that pinched his face and accentuated the puffs under his eyes as he towered above the podium. It was the accumulated weariness of days and nights and years of living and giving and working as if his superhuman energies were endless. It was the secret fear that haunts the creator, the fear which tormented Sherwood, in spite of his confidence, that his gift had left him because of his not having had a successful new play produced on Broadway in fourteen years.

It was the sorrow and the emptiness of the letdown after the death of Roosevelt and after the dizzying tensions and excitements of the war years spent close to the White House and to great events. It was the heartbreak of seeing the heroic efforts and sacrifices of a second world war end in disenchantment, with Hitler and the other marchers stopped, but with victory not even bringing a true peace. It was the deep alarm with which he recognized the threats of nuclear power and his realization that this time he spoke not only in a different world but, again, in a different age.

Sherwood had tried to tell the unflinching truth as he saw

and felt it in 1940 when Paris had fallen. He tried to do the same thing now as, with his long, nervous fingers spilling communication, he opened his manuscript and began to read, having put on his reading glasses.

He was seeking to pay tribute to and to justify the war dead at a frightening and frightened time. The needs of peace had long brought unprotesting acceptance of the country's first peacetime conscription. Unrest and menace were everywhere. The once veiled language of diplomacy had become an open rivalry in invective. Old empires were tottering and slumbering continents awakening. Nationalism was once again a panacea. Dien Bien Phu was about to fall. An uneasy truce existed in Korea.

The Cold War was always hot. The balance of power had been replaced by the balance of terror. The United States had been catapulted into a pre-eminence among the free nations that it did not want, did not like, and was not as yet equipped to occupy. Soviet might was catching up with Soviet bluster. The death struggle between Communism and Capitalism was a phrase on many tongues and a fact dreaded though accepted by most minds. McCarthyism was at its ugly height, and within ten days "point of order . . . point of order" was to be heard on the air with the insistent buzz of a pneumatic drill in an idiot's hands, as the junior Senator from Wisconsin intimidated the Army before television cameras just as in public and in private he had intimidated the Administration and millions of Americans. Due to the atmosphere of fear McCarthy epitomized, J. Robert Oppenheimer had been badgered and bullied before the Gray Board in a proceeding in which few could take pride. It was not a comfortable moment at which to speak of the fruits of victory made possible by the sacrifices of the gallant dead. Nor did Sherwood minimize the darkness of the hour.

The valedictorian of eighteen was now the elder statesman of fifty-eight, and spoke as one. Arms and the man was his theme—the new arms, the new America, the new Russia, and the new age—and his plea, in the name of survival, was for a war on war. His was a long, discursive speech, prepared to fill that obligatory hour which is the common expectation and tolerance of an audience that has come to hear a "lecture." Though poorly organized and somewhat tired, it made its telling points, showed in many passages Sherwood's facile expository skill, and was blessed with fervor. It found Sherwood, again like his own Dr. Valkonen in a threatened schoolroom, still speaking as an idealist of the jungle world outside but this time asserting with more hope than confidence that there shall be no night.

Once again he turned back to the lost tranquillity of 1914, when to young Americans "major war was something that was buried in the cemetery at Gettysburg," and putting on uniforms to fight was unthinkable. He referred to 1940, too, pointing out that there was one piece of news which he had not mentioned when Paris fell because he had not known it, and which he could not have mentioned if he had. On the day after his Commencement address, Franklin Roosevelt had at the White House signed an order to Dr. Vannevar Bush authorizing him "to study into the possible relationship to national defense of recent discoveries in the field of atomistics, notably the fission of uranium." That was the beginning of the new age, and, as Sherwood said, by 1954 the A-bomb had already become "antiquated."

As a militant pacifist in the years following Wilson's failure at Versailles, he deplored the folly of high-minded pacifism and disarmament that had only made possible the rise of the dictators in Germany, Italy, Japan, and Russia. He quoted at length from an ignored three weeks' old article in the New York *Times* by William L. Laurence on the cobalt bomb and the life-taking radioactive dust it was capable of spreading for thousands of miles across lands and oceans. He stressed the futility of outlawing the worst of weapons, insisting that we face up to the fact that "war is a dirty business and those who engage in it must be prepared and even eager to fight it in the dirtiest manner possible," never forgetting that world disarmament is the ultimate goal.

Once more he apologized for the "shocking unpleasant subjects" he had felt compelled to discuss, and with manifest effort tried to rise above doom as he had written Mr. Perry that he would. "Every major challenge," said he, "that has been hurled at our people has been met and greatly met," and those who died meeting these challenges did not die in vain. From Milton's Honor Roll he singled out three names that had for him "a particular emotional meaning." From the First War he cited Charlie Reynolds, the head monitor of his class in 1914; from the Second, his own brother's son, Philip Burr Sherwood; and from the Korean War, the son of an old and dear friend, George Lee.

His conclusion, though by obligation hortatory, was bound to be inconclusive. It was, "We have the strength, if only we assert it." The strong faith was qualified, the "if only" insistently strong. Sherwood needed to believe, and still believed, but his beliefs were sorely tried. He spoke as a man made melancholy by the spectacle of human folly and the terrible and needless possibilities of doom brought about by a progress that was in so many ways retrogressive. He spoke as a man seeking to believe in Man in the age of the thermonuclear bomb, "the instrument of extermination."

He spoke as someone who, as he saw the darkness deepen in the postwar years, had considered it "a privilege to escape from the appalling and inexplicable present" and to relive the confident greatness of the war years by writing *Roosevelt and Hopkins*. He spoke as a man too aware of the threats of the new age not to be sad in a world that had changed almost beyond knowing since the sunnily secure days of his youth and childhood.

In three speeches delivered in the same place over a span of forty years, Sherwood had supplied a rough chart of his times and of the challenges with which he had lived and from which he had written.

STEWART'S, COLORADO SPRINGS

WATER

The Wine of Architecture

Sparkling or still, its ability to enhance

a building has been appreciated for centuries—

but the sixties look to be vintage years

By ADA LOUISE HUXTABLE

Pools and jets echo the long horizontals and sharp verticals of the dining hall at the U.S. Air Force Academy in Colorado Springs

There is, perhaps, no more solid, stable, and material art than architecture, and no more ethereal, evanescent, and volatile element than water. When the two combine, it is for effects of singular magnificence and mystery. Water is spirit to architecture's substance; it is the wine, wit, and grace of building; feminine quicksilver to masculine sobriety; jewel trim for sober stone in sparkling sprays and jets; narcissistic sheets of silver for architecture's solemn beauties. Its fountains, cascades, channels, and pools are the supreme aesthetic *grand geste* that has traditionally completed the greatest building schemes of every age.

Every age, that is, until our own, because the twentieth century has been uniquely dry. The reforms of modern architecture left neither room nor taste for superfluous watery joys. Like another great dry experiment of our time, however, this also has come to an end; a revival that began as a trickle in the fifties, with timid sprays and bubblings, promises to become a magnificent splash in the sixties, as we re-embrace the subtleties and glories of designing with water for a renaissance of the grand aqueous art.

The use of water with architecture has a long history and a universally seductive appeal. "Water-works," as the artful disposition of still and moving water has been called at least since the Renaissance, have been less concerned with plumbing than with pleasure. Their primary purpose has been to provide delight, drama, and conspicuous display—three nonessentials that nourish the spirit of man. Water may slake his thirst or, in today's buildings, even supply his air conditioners, but it can do so quite well without the flourish of fountains and falls. Whether it takes the form of an extravagant baroque torrent or a serene Oriental pool, the character of water is primarily sensuous, and its pleasures are visual and auditory. It adds extra dimensions—motion, sound, and the manipulation of light—to the customarily static three dimensions of building. It is a performance and a show. Its playful, changeable range runs from the breathtakingly theatrical to the mysteriously subtle. It is capable of broad jokes and tenuous elegancies. Above all, it is an unparalleled instrument of grandeur and romance.

Because it is so often nonfunctional, water is the one de-

sign element with which the architect can be singularly free. A pretty pond, a fortuitous lake, a cleverly incorporated stream, may be a bonus and even radically alter his scheme, but he must bring them into existence to make them qualify as examples of this highly arbitrary and artificial art. Its sources are nature, but its naturalness is artifice. It is meant to charm, to please, to impress, to startle, to titillate, and to offer myriad sensations and surprises. Its deeper implications suggest evanescent joys, cleansing of the spirit, the transience of perfection, the insubstantiality of dreams, the flowing continuity of life, and a consummate, fleeting beauty—impermanent, like all great romantic beauties, and therefore more beautiful than the tangible and real.

In its greatest expressions, water transcends and transforms architecture. The Piazza Navona in Rome did not become a classic example of a great urban architectural space until the open plaza and all of its buildings were given scale, focus, and meaning by Bernini's magnificently exuberant Fountain of the Four Rivers in the seventeenth century (see page 20), and until the statuary and basins of the two side fountains were completed in the following years. At Versailles there is a bosquet, or clump of trees, arranged as an open-air ballroom (see above); an architectural space hollowed out of nature, its stepped walls were defined originally by cascades, with dry tiers of seats for musicians and observers and a marble dance floor at its base for the king and his court. On occasion, water even becomes a kind of architecture, in a fascinating and calculated confusion of effects. The famous water gardens of the Villa d'Este at Tivoli (see pages 18–19) so mix arches, walls, niches, gates, and porticoes with sprays and falls that a decorative, freestanding, aquatic architecture is created, of which water is an inseparable part. Cascades at the Villa Aldobrandini at Frascati (see above, right), winding down columns and becoming broad sheets of carefully defined and maintained shape, approached—quite consciously—an almost architectural solidity. To add to the deliberate deception, trees and hedges were trimmed geometrically to make flat, high, green, out-door walls that would have delighted that modern master of beautiful walls-for-their-own-sake, Mies van der Rohe.

To the ancients, the magic of water was more than aesthetic. The fountain of Hippocrene appeared where the winged Pegasus had struck his hoof, and because the nymph Salmacis, protector of the spring of Caria, had indulged in an unhappy love affair with Hermaphroditus, those who drank of the fountain's waters became effeminate. If the Greeks emphasized miracle and myth, the Romans, more practical, put water to better uses. In the atriums of their houses, pools and fountains soothed the senses and served domestic needs. Their monumental baths turned simple cleanliness into a sumptuous ritual in an equally sumptuous setting.

Later, when the secrets of materialistic comfort, like indoor piping, were lost or forgotten, the water supply retired to the street. The medieval street fountain became a combined plumbing utility, work of art, social center, and focus of the town square. They were lovely things, these fountains, intimately scaled miniature works of architecture reflecting pinnacled Gothic building patterns in the north or taking the form of low, stepped basins in Italy and the south, often adorned with ingenuous figures and reliefs, their fall of water modest and sufficient for both pleasure and utility. The restored Gothic Schöner Brunnen in Nuremberg, the charming medieval fountains of Aix, the thirteenth-century creations at Viterbo in Italy, are all examples of this genre. One of the most famous is the Fonte Maggiore of Perugia, executed by the Pisanos in 1278, a work celebrated in every fine-arts textbook as a moment of inspired architectural and sculptural transition between medieval and modern.

The Renaissance continued this type of architectural town fountain, classicizing its motifs and carrying its familiar forms to new heights of grace, grandeur, and sophistication. In the sixteenth century, with the flowering of figure sculpture, appeared those glistening, dripping gods, heroes, and maidens—spurting, spraying, and pouring water—

Today's architects often try to bring the outdoors inside, but in the seventeenth and eighteenth centuries it was the other way around. Water and vegetation were used to create open-air salons that were simply greener, moister counterparts of those in the palace itself. Examples are the Salle de Bal set in a bosquet at Versailles (opposite) and the wonderful cascade at the Villa Aldobrandini in Italy (right).

that have set the character and clichés of fountain design until the present day. At the same time, the public fountain took on more of the independent stature of a work of art, largely sculptural, and became in the process somewhat detached from its environment.

The sixteenth century also promoted, and eventually discarded, one of the most magnificent and intriguing uses of water with building in the history of architecture: the French Renaissance châteaux of the Valois kings, a group of monarchs who suffered conspicuously from bouts of *maladie de bâtir* cured only by the construction of new palaces on a megalomaniac scale. If the king craved a little simple hunting, a complex of Gargantuan super blocks was promptly erected in the countryside, and if he tired of one castle, he built another. Water was an important part of most of these ambitious schemes. Most often the design called for the château to be surrounded by an artificially created moat in the medieval tradition, but broader, grander, and purely ornamental, in keeping with expanding Renaissance tastes. There was usually a "channel-garden," with a central canal considerably larger than the later, famous lagoon at Versailles. So grandiose were the plans, and so expensive their execution and maintenance, that the aquatic embellishments were not always carried out, or did not long survive.

The stylish façade of Francis I's Chambord, for example, was to have been completely encircled with water, requiring special canalization of the Cosson River. This decorative moat was never finished, and in the eighteenth century it was filled in and the river rediverted. In Bernard Palissy's executed works for Cardinal Bourbon at Gaillon and Catherine de Médicis at Chenonceaux, castles and artificial islands projected from watery settings; streams, channels, and *allées* crossed each other primly and led to rocky grottoes with reptile-stocked pools, for an odd and undoubtedly appealing mixture of sensuousness and sentiment, of medieval romanticism and Renaissance rationalism.

But the Renaissance was only a curtain raiser for the

baroque. The seventeenth century was the Age of Water, and the fantasies of the Italian *seicento* make all other aquatic achievements pale beside them. The exuberance, the orgiastic display, the emotional extravagance, the impassioned overstatement of the baroque taste, turned naturally to a medium that offered maximum excitement, drama, and change. Paradoxically, we admire most what we would not, today, dare to create. The fantastic water gardens of the sixteenth and seventeenth centuries of the Villa d'Este at Tivoli, the Boboli Gardens in Florence, the Villas Aldobrandini at Frascati and Torlonia at Porto, the fountains of the Villa Lante at Bagnaia—all stressed exaggerated flights of fancy, united the beautiful and the grotesque with suave assurance, piled drama on drama, and capped climax with climax to produce effects that remain among the most marvelous artistic achievements of any age.

The ideals of the baroque were dynamic movement and superhuman grandeur. Against a background of building elements progressively related to the great houses—porticoes, walls, arcades, columns, gates, stairs, and platforms on a series of stepped levels—an infinite variety of water forms, including jets, streams, sprays, pools, fountains, and cascades, were integrated with that rare, stylish synthesis which characterized the baroque talent and has escaped every period since.

But it is the elaborate and imaginative use of sculpture that makes these waterworks unique. No purist theories, no shackles of "good taste," held the baroque artist back. At the Villa d'Este alone, a conservative inventory of sculptural elements, used independently or in architectural compositions, but used always with water, yields a formidable assortment of gods and goddesses with mythological entourages; boats, obelisks, eagles, dolphins, horses, wolves; fanciful rock groups; maidens standing, sitting, and reclining; small boys relieving themselves from high pedestals; masks, *putti*, and shells. The famous water organ, which played a tune as water pressure forced air through pipes, was a popular conceit of the time. Even more popular were

the "water jokes," a source of hilarious amusement to their aristocratic perpetrators, causing unwary visitors to be doused by pipes concealed in benches, steps, and trees, or wherever they would cause the most delicious embarrassment. The Villa's water needs, of course, could have been supplied in far simpler fashion, but the water garden ran the gamut from fun house to gallery of art.

Order, however, was the other side of the baroque coin, and behind the uninhibited displays was a carefully prescribed plan. The design of the house, garden, and water system followed a formal, co-ordinated pattern. Water courses and fountains were used as instruments of the new science of perspective, to lead the eye through symmetrical vistas. It is water, also, that gives unity to the city of Rome, through its fountains, particularly as they appear in the seventeenth-century masterpieces of Giovanni Lorenzo Bernini, which remain in the nostalgic mind's eye and ear as the embodiment of the city's voluptuous spirit. The visitor who has lingered late in the Piazza Navona will always remember the sounds of the early Roman evening, the muted splashing and murmuring of great fountains as their Gargantuan figures are bathed in deepening golden light. Rome is the sound of running water, and Bernini's fountains are its heart.

As the baroque moved north to conquer Europe, the French raised it to a cooler, more intellectual grandeur and gave the world Versailles. But first, in 1661, they built Vaux-le-Vicomte, the one-thousand-acre estate of Nicolas Fouquet, finance minister of Louis XIV. It was erected in a style of such striking splendor that the King, jealous of its magnificence and suspicious of its costs, ordered Fouquet arrested shortly after the spectacular opening fete given by the minister in his honor. By a curious coincidence, Louis had something similar in mind, and soon the designers of Vaux-le-Vicomte, including the architect-trained André Le Nôtre who created the gardens that dazzled the world, were in the King's employ, building Versailles.

Le Nôtre took the formal baroque plan and the seventeenth-century love affair with water and defined them both with unprecedented elegance. Glittering sprays, placid pools, and wide green parterres were carefully related to the massive marble buildings. The Grand Canal that stretches beyond the Basin of Apollo on the main axis of the palace was large enough to accommodate a miniature fleet and a permanent delegation of Venetian gondoliers. The leafy bosquets were punctuated by flashing fountains and water fancies that included sparkling plumes arching over dry walks, artificial rain delicately falling on trees and grasses made of copper, and a water theatre where, according to a contemporary witness, "the water goes through many and diverse changes . . . and its play causes as much surprise as admiration."

These hydraulic marvels were engineered by François and Pierre de Francine, who constructed a system of "water machines"—horse pumps and windmills—to bring water to the palace reservoirs (the supply became so scanty as the works grew that most of the next decade was spent in seeking additional sources). Faced with the further demands of the Trianon Gardens in 1670, the Francines devised, probably in desperation, a way to recirculate and re-use the inadequate supplies.

The principles of Le Nôtre and the Francines were carried to England in 1712 in a curious and delightful book, *The Theory and Practice of Gardening*, John James's translation of Dezallier d'Argenville's classic French treatise on the design of grounds and waterworks in the manner of Versailles. England already had the "exquisite waterworks" of the first phase of Chatsworth, including the Great Cascade, the Neptune Fountains, and the copper weeping willow, which were in construction as early as 1687. Together with the bird-song grotto at Wilton, where unwary bird lovers were suitably saturated, these had left Englishmen avid for more. James recommended "Basons and large Pieces of Water" with appropriate water forms: "Cascades, Gullets, Buffets, Sheets, Masks, Bubbles, Mushrooms, Sheafs, Spouts, Surges,

Candlesticks, Grills, Tapers, Crosses, and vaulted Arches," to be accompanied by "Maritime Ornaments . . . Congelations, Petrifyings, and Shell-Works, Water-Leaves, Bulrushes and Reeds . . . and Figures that naturally belong to the Water, as Rivers, Naiades or Water Nymphs, Tritons, Serpents, Sea-Horses, Dragons, Dolphins, Griffins, and Frogs, which are made to throw out and vomit Streams and Torrents of Water."

In the eighteenth century, "Congelations, Petrifyings, Spouts, and Surges" appeared all over Europe. The construction of that superb, perennially popular, aquatic attraction of Rome, the Fountain of Trevi—the work of Nicola Salvi from 1732–62—was financed by popular lotteries and accompanied by outraged public cries as expenses mounted. Peterhof, the show place of the Russian Czars (see page 25), was begun c. 1716 by Jean-Baptiste Le Blond, Le Nôtre's illustrious pupil; and Caserta, the formidable creation of Charles III of Naples (see page 21), was built in the years after 1752 by Luigi and Carlo Vanvitelli and an impressive assortment of sculptors, engineers, and artisans. Called, respectively, the Russian and Italian Versailles, they shared the characteristic of all later versions of a monumental stylistic achievement: their conception was bigger, but not better. By one of the delightful ironies of history, the hydraulic high jinks of the Romanovs, containing, by official U.S.S.R. count, approximately 2,500 pipes, is now Communist-maintained, even to a loyal Soviet worker whose sole duty it is to turn the cock for unsuspected drenchings by the "water surprises."

In England the change to a romantic naturalism in landscape design in the later eighteenth century put a temporary end to artificial displays. The nineteenth century was preoccupied with plumbing, but the taste for grandeur returned momentarily with the waterworks of the famous London Crystal Palace of 1851—so much more expensive than the building itself that they threatened the Exposition with bankruptcy and signaled the end of a long, aqueous road.

While Western civilization concerned itself with water in motion, the aquatic embellishments of the buildings and gardens of the East had followed a different course. Their designers would have been surprised to know, as John James decreed to the English, that "flat Water . . . being always quiet and in the same State . . . is no great Beauty." The beauty they sought was gentle and placid. The effects they created were artfully natural and heavy with symbolism in the carefully constructed garden ponds and lakes of China and Japan; quietly evocative in the flat, reflecting sheets of Mogul palaces and tombs; and solemnly impressive in the great temple tanks of India (see page 27), where the rivers, considered messengers of God, were diverted for the double purpose of purification and divine communication. No monumental sprays or falls disturbed the calculated serenity or the harmonious relationship of building and image, of the tangible and the unreal. Moving water in the East traveled without bombast, through calm channels or down gently inclined, carved marble slabs. Nor has anyone understood better the concentrated psychological effectiveness of a single crystal-clear jet bubbling from a small silver lotus, or a shallow stream flowing softly through a garden court.

At the same time that Italian torrents were reaching their roaring apogee, the architecture of the sixteenth and seventeenth centuries in northern India had developed a water art of quiet elegance; marble monuments, like the classic Taj Mahal at Agra, were mirrored in man-made lagoons, so that substance merged with shimmering reflection. The Red Fort at Delhi by Shah Jahan incorporated water in one of the most remarkable architectural compositions ever realized: it flowed through the center of open courts and roofed pavilions as a series of flat streams and pools, sometimes exposed, sometimes underground; murmurous and light-reflecting, it was the building's soul.

The lesson of Eastern ways with water—of simplicity, subtlety, and sensuous understatement—was brought to the West by the Moorish invasions; most notably in the exquisite, delicately conceived water courts of the fourteenth-

15

century Alhambra in Spain (see page 26). Significantly, the current revival of water in architecture is closer to the principles and practices of the East than to the traditions of the West. Moreover, there is a recognizable pattern of taste and technique in this new use of water—the kind of consistency that binds the best work of any period into a coherent whole, which we may call a style. In current American and European examples there are fountains and pools, but instead of the unbridled exuberance of earlier centuries, we have enrichment with restraint. Rather than an all-out assault on the senses, there is an understated, almost Oriental suggestiveness. Serene instead of spectacular, it uses a kind of calm classicism to promote timeless, romantic images. Thus, the still reflecting pool, hallmark of the East, lends its evocative subtlety to a surprising and unexpected assortment of contemporary structures: office buildings, embassies, universities, houses, and factories. As in the Orient, the water itself is stressed, usually eliminating sculpture. While it may be useful, it is just as often purely ornamental—the beguiling nonessential that water in architecture has always been.

Edward Durrell Stone, one of the chief proponents of this aesthetic extra, acknowledges his debt to Mogul architecture in the reflecting pool for his handsome American Embassy at New Delhi, and employs sprays and jets of water with a lavish romantic hand inside and outside of manufacturing plants, exposition buildings, and private houses. The Connecticut General Life Insurance Company headquarters in Bloomfield, Connecticut, by Skidmore, Owings & Merrill, includes pond-gardens with round, flooded slabs by sculptor Isamu Noguchi, and the same firm's new administration center for the Upjohn Company in Kalamazoo, Michigan, has a series of intimate, pool-studded interior courts. Minoru Yamasaki, an architect who displays an exceptional awareness of the psychological and aesthetic contrasts of water and structure (see pages 32–33), has set his McGregor Center at Wayne State University in Detroit in a pool with floating platforms and bridge approaches. His Reynolds Metals building is water-surrounded, and the new Detroit Gas Company headquarters will be entered over a lily-strewn moat. Eero Saarinen's buildings for the General Motors Technical Center near Detroit are perhaps the first large-scale modern revival of water-focused architecture, and the water court of his Oslo Embassy is one of the handsomest interiors of recent years. Philip Johnson has installed a 120-foot *jet d'eau* on his own grounds, for his own pleasure, and in the best *grand siècle* tradition plans a decorative pavilion beneath the spray.

Johnson's fountain is more prophetic than reactionary, for there is a growing interest in water in motion, and architects are turning once more to sprays, jets, and falls. A new vocabulary has been made available by two modern inventions—the submersible pump, which brings up water directly from pipes in the bottom of a pool or installation, eliminating the necessity of having the source at a higher level to insure pressure for fountains or sprays; and electronic controls, which permit abstract patterns of water to be recorded on tape and later played and replayed like music. (All of the remarkable effects of earlier centuries were achieved, surprisingly, by gravity.) According to Johnson, who is at work on a $200,000 fountain for New York City's Lincoln Center, we will see increasing emphasis on movement, mass, and height. There will be color: Lincoln Center will have gold and silver lights at night. There will be tricks: dramatic cutoffs will catch the fifty-foot aerated spray at the top of its flight—"Look, no feet!" says Johnson —then let it shower down in brilliant, floodlit drops before the next surge. Seattle features a prize-winning example of this type at its Century 21 Exposition this year, to be kept as a permanent civic center installation, and the 1964 New York World's Fair plans spectacular displays. This will be modern water theatre in the grand manner of Versailles.

And so, the twentieth century promises to join two great traditions—that of the West, which treats water like fire, and of the East, which likens it to love. Its tenuous, enigmatic union with architecture has been given poetic permanence in an Arabic inscription on one of the Alhambra's fountains: "Look at the water and look at the basin, and you will not be able to tell if it is the water that is motionless or the marble which ripples. Like the prisoner of love whose face is full of trouble and fear when under the gaze of the envious, so the jealous water is indignant at the marble, and the marble is envious of the water." It has been a long-lasting, passionate affair.

Ada Louise Huxtable, Contributing Editor for architecture to the New York Times *and author of a new guide to New York's modern architecture, has previously written about street furniture and world's fairs for* HORIZON.

Water Makes the Difference

On the following pages: a portfolio of its delights

This cast-iron fountain with its spreading skirts of water stands in the little town of Sézanne, east of Paris. Both it and the church behind it, Gothic inside and routine baroque on the outside, are hastily passed over by the guidebooks: neither is expected to interest the traveler. Nor would they, perhaps, standing alone. But the arching pattern of the water lends grace to the stiff façade of the church; the massiveness of the latter makes the fountain seem more fragile than it is; and together these anonymous and not very distinctive monuments create the kind of European cityscape that beguiles the tourist from America, where water is regularly put to work but seldom allowed to play in the streets.

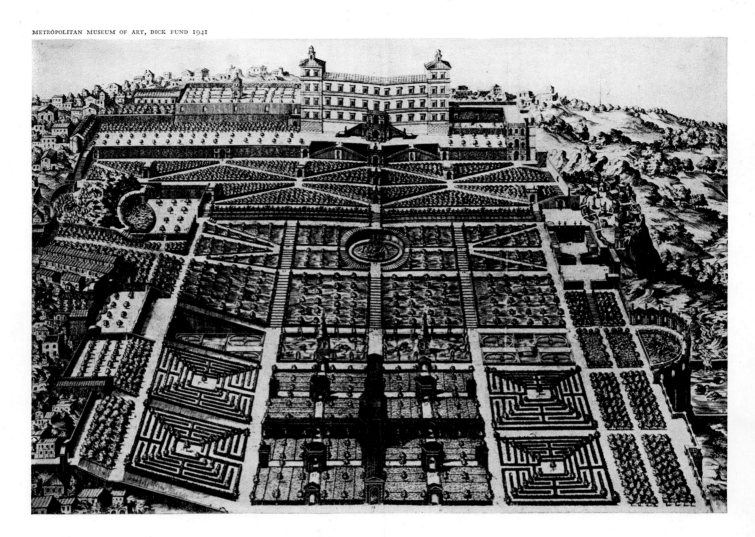

18

Water has rarely been used more extravagantly than in the famous gardens of the Villa d'Este, sixteen miles east of Rome, where the capacities of the medium for ornamental effects have been pushed almost as far as they will go. From some five hundred fountains it gushes, spurts, sprays, and spills into pools and channels through which it further cascades, tumbles, races, or—rarely—is allowed to pause. These gardens were begun in the mid-sixteenth century by the Cardinal Ippolito II d'Este, who, having five times failed in his attempts to be elected pope, decided nevertheless to live in pontifical splendor. The engraving above, dated 1573, shows what was probably the original design, although some of its elements were not carried out and many others have since been changed. Cutting across the plan just above its central circular basin is the Alley of the Hundred Fountains (left)—today there are ninety-one—a three-level arrangement of jets, fans, sprays, and spillovers now heavily overgrown with maidenhair fern. But the most spectacular display is the Fountain of the Water Organ (opposite), with jets of varying heights to simulate organ pipes. The organ itself, an ingenious hydraulic model, was housed in the structure at the top, but its repertoire was limited to one tune only.

Dripping Gods and Goddesses

Rome is murmurous with fountains; indeed, one is never far from the sound of running water or from the sight of mossy marble deities reclining in the spray— whether they are the naiads of the Piazza dell'Esedra (right) or the river gods on Bernini's Fountain of the Four Rivers in the old Piazza Navona (opposite). The god shown here personifies the Ganges; others represent the Nile, the Danube, and the Rio de la Plata. For more agitated tableaux one has to go south to Caserta, where the grandiose eighteenth-century palace of the kings of Naples provides scenes like that above. Diana (center) has just discovered Actaeon spying on her and her maidens while they bathe. For this faux pas she changed him into a stag, and he was torn to pieces by his own hounds—a fate depicted with similar vivacity to the left of the cascade.

Fountains of Physiology

Seventeenth-century ingenuity in the manipulation of water led, perhaps inevitably, to such dubious conceits as those shown here. The grotesque masks spewing water from nostrils (opposite) or mouth (top
right) and the shameless sphinx (bottom center) are all at the Villa
d'Este. The Triton (top left), the face below it, and the spitting lion
adorn Roman fountains. Most famous of all is the Manneken-Pis of Brussels (bottom right), which stands near the city hall. Beside these salivat-
ing, lactating, and micturating specimens of the fountain designer's art,
the Balinese maidens (bottom left) show an admirable Oriental restraint.

DUNCAN EDWARDS—FPG

Fountains As Royal Status Symbols

The arrogance of high-flung jets of water understandably appealed to absolute monarchs like Peter the Great of Russia and Ludwig II of Bavaria, who ruled with similar defiance of the laws of political gravity. The array of cascades and jets at Peterhof (above), the summer palace Peter built about 1720, is not only a supremely showy use of water but a direct expression of regal magnificence. Today it presumably expresses just Russian magnificence, for it is kept in immaculate repair by the Soviet government and is a favorite excursion spot for Sunday trippers from nearby Leningrad. Schloss Linderhof (opposite), also a tourist attraction, was built by Ludwig to satisfy his unbridled passion for rococo—one might say for unbridled rococo—and with its writhing interiors and tortured gardens it was, in the 1870's, at least a hundred years behind the times. But the solitary jet rising ninety feet from its basin is genuinely impressive, and as insolent in its challenge to the surrounding mountains as Ludwig's efforts to emulate Louis XIV in the nineteenth century.

25

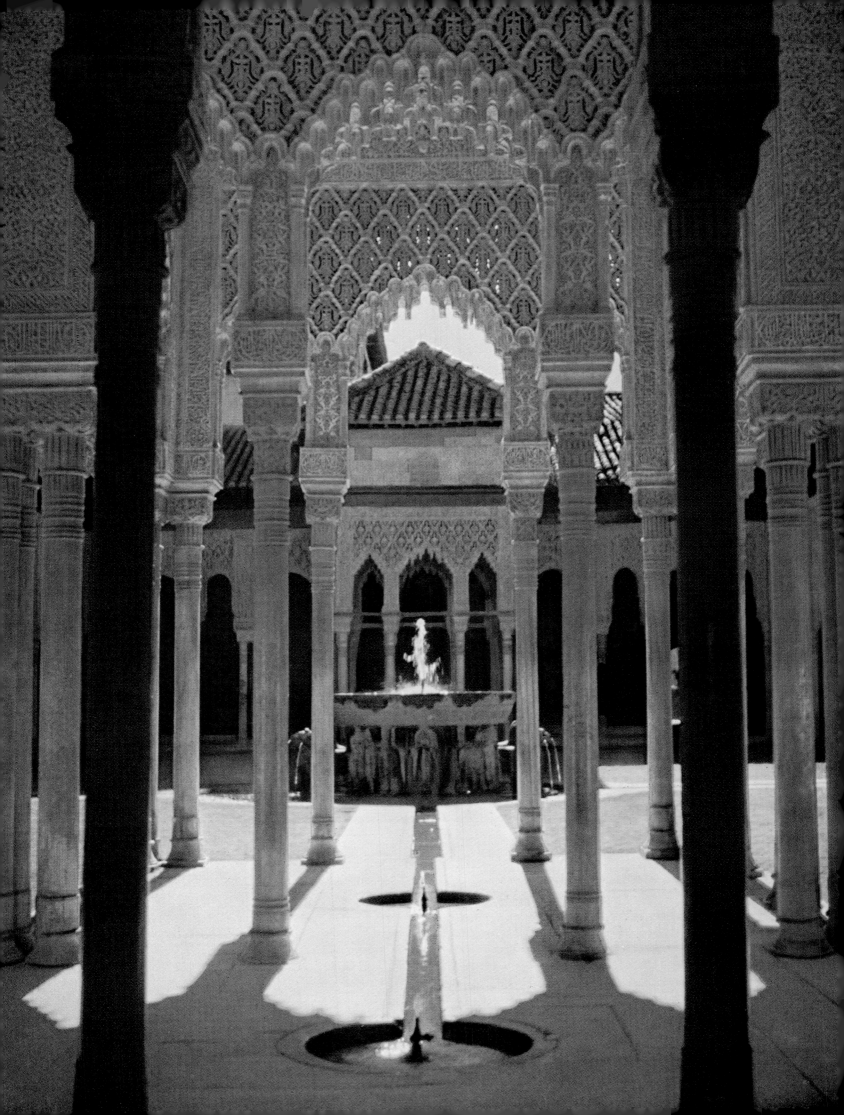

The Quiet Waters of Asia

The flashy fountains of the West have no counterpart in the East, where water is too sacred—or too scarce—for extravagant display. Every mosque has its basin for ritualistic ablutions, just as every Moslem garden has its pool or tiny jet; but they make do with the thinnest trickle of water, magnifying it by the stoniness of tiled courtyards and pavements. Even when Islam moved west it took its spare, aqueous aesthetic with it and produced in Spain, after the Moorish conquest, such masterpieces as the Court of the Lions in the Alhambra (opposite). Built in the fourteenth century and intended to be of the utmost splendor, it attains its effect with a relatively small amount of water—indicating both the rareness of this commodity (Spain is almost as arid as the Middle East) and the delicacy of the conception. Water was equally necessary for the ablutions of the Hindus. But with more of it at hand, they were able to spread it about more lavishly, as in the temple tanks at Jambukeshwar in south India (above). The tank is also an important element in Indian secular architecture, where its surface is often dotted with elegant man-made islets in the form of kiosks or fountains like the one shown at right. Standing in the women's quarters of a Jodhpur palace, it is thought to commemorate some princely forebear.

The Northern Way With Water

The twentieth-century fountain revival began somewhat earlier in Scandinavia than it did in southern Europe. The foremost fountain designer of our day is the late Swedish-born sculptor Carl Milles, who spent twenty-one years at Cranbrook Academy in Michigan. There he installed a variation of his Orpheus fountain (left), eight delicately poised figures standing in a circle. In the original version, designed for the Stockholm Music Hall, they surrounded a statue of Orpheus—but at Cranbrook, Orpheus has been left out. The eight figures, Milles said, "are not symbolic; they are just people listening to music. The only real figure in it is Beethoven" (above). Milles represented a talented last gasp of the Renaissance tradition, which also accounts for Dyre Vaa's swan fountain (right) outside Oslo's Town Hall. But contemporary water architecture, especially in America, owes much more to the still-water traditions of the Orient.

At Home With Water

BALTAZAR KORAB

COURTESY LOUISIANA

BALTAZAR KORAB

The house that architect Alden Dow has built for himself in Midland, Michigan (above), emerges from the surrounding water like a low-lying island—an illusion heightened by the approach over a camel-back bridge (far left). In the study, just to the right of the birch tree, the shimmering surface of the pond is at window-sill— and eye—level. Where Dow has used water to create a picturesque exterior setting, Edward D. Stone has used it to create an extraordinary interior. In the house he designed for Mr. and Mrs. Bruno Graf of Dallas (right), the dining area is a circular slab of marble seemingly afloat on an illuminated pool. Not domestic architecture, but domestic in scale—in keeping with its setting in the park of an old country house —is the little pool with steppingstones (left) leading to a wing of the new Louisiana Museum located outside Copenhagen.

IVAN MASSER—BLACK STAR

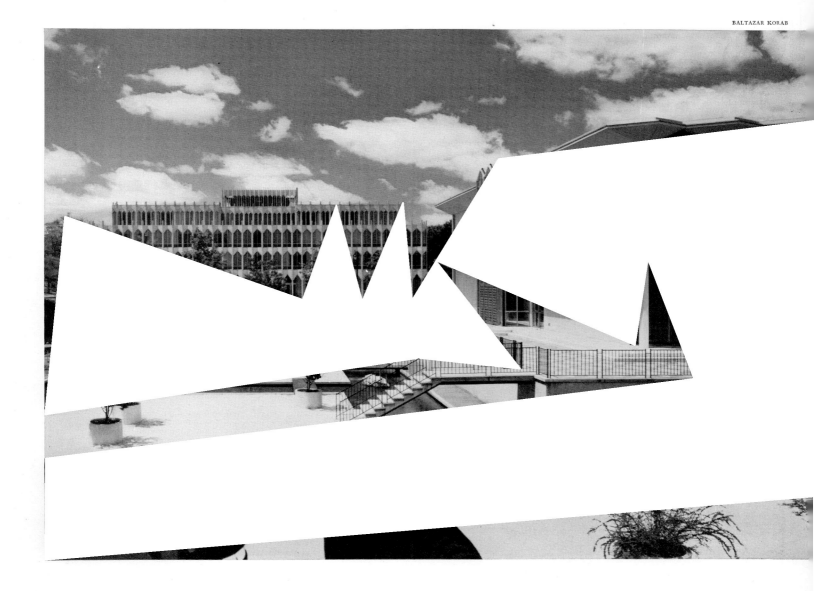

East, West—Which is Best?

Ornamental water in contemporary architecture owes more to Eastern subtlety than to past Western flamboyance. The Detroit architect Minoru Yamasaki, whose buildings are not otherwise notably Oriental in feeling, likes to place them on podiums and surround them with reflecting pools that often contain lily pads or artificial islands. Two examples in Detroit are his Regional Sales Office for the Reynolds Metals Company (opposite) and the McGregor Center at Wayne State University (above). Baroque-like turbulence, on the other hand, characterizes the new waterscape at the Deering Milliken textile plant in Spartanburg, S.C. (right). Faced with the problem of cooling water for a vast air-conditioning system, the firm of Skidmore, Owings & Merrill solved it by setting recirculating sprays and jets of varying heights in a decorative pool.

THE MAN IN THE IRONIC MASK

By BURTON HERSH

Inventor of a new kind of theatre, foremost play-wright of Communist Europe, virtuoso of guile in a world he treated as a jungle, the late Bertolt Brecht turned against the middle-class self-satis-faction of his elders with a savagery that still reverberates. During Brecht on Brecht, *a recently performed program of extracts from his writings and speeches, Brecht's sardonic photograph (be-low) smiles down on Lotte Lenya—a link to the prewar German stage where they both were bred.*

We are at last well into our Brecht boom. The late German revolutionary playwright, poet, and iconoclast of stagecraft, after finally having broken through in America with seven sizzling years of the off-Broadway production of his *Threepenny Opera*, has taken root in the repertory of New York's Living Theatre * with his early paean to the manic cravings of the twenties, *In the Jungle of Cities*; and that house now plans to introduce still another early Brecht play, *Man Is Man*. Washington's Arena Stage Theatre opened its doors in 1961 with a theatre-in-the-round presentation of his *Caucasian Chalk Circle*; New York radio stations have scheduled rebroadcasts of peripheral Brecht contributions to opera and ballet; *Brecht on Brecht*, an evening of readings from his works, has been running at New York's Theatre de Lys; and to signify Brecht's elevation to that state of absolute grace known as Potential Box Office, his *Mr. Puntila and His Hired Man, Matti*, his *Mother Courage*, his *Resistible Rise of Arturo Ui* are expected on Broadway itself. Before long, Brecht is likely to become the most successful avowed Communist playwright in America.

Such posthumous success has been a long and uncertain time coming. To some extent Bertolt Brecht's rising reputation here has been fired by his recognition in Europe. His own Berliner Ensemble, the repertory company founded under his direction in East Berlin in the late 1940's, has triumphed too often in the major European capitals to be ignored. More significantly, the enthusiasm here for Brecht seems to have originated and gained its force in the boondocks of the American theatrical world: on the experimental stages of assorted college campuses. And behind the whole movement—functioning not only as translator but as methodologist, director, propagandist, and number-one disciple of Brecht in America—has been Eric Bentley, of Columbia University, teacher and critic of drama and editor of numerous anthologies. In a note to his translation of some choice Brecht plays, Bentley explains: "Both . . . were produced in the United States as early as 1948, the initiative stemming from ex-students of mine who were by then directors of college theatres. Thereafter both of the plays became part of the repertoire of the more wide-awake campus theatres."

So much for *how* Brecht began to proselytize at the grass roots. *Why* is more complicated. Certainly, Brecht—a naturally austere and fundamentalist but highly explosive talent—appeals spontaneously to the iconoclasm of college students. They have less to unlearn than their elders; and so Brecht's naked stage and his few weathered props, his unashamed didacticism and his revolutionary notions about acting technique, provide them with a useful starting point.

Bertolt Brecht himself has been dead nearly six years now; were he still alive, the situation would very likely provoke his tight ironic smile. One way or another, the United States held a perennial fascination for Brecht, and his attitude toward this country developed through two distinct stages. First, when Brecht was still the boy revolutionary of the German theatre, he liked to portray America as the cockpit of capitalistic barbarism; later, when he had fled from Nazi Germany and settled in Santa Monica between 1941 and

1948, he stopped writing about America and tried to come to personal terms with it. Early and late, Brecht was misguided; he failed in both attempts and for the same reason: he was too profoundly German. When he thought he was writing about the United States, he really was projecting his vision of the worst in German society. When, later, he tried to impress American motion-picture producers or theatre audiences, more often than not he resorted to ferocious stage ideas or a style that could not be transplanted from the Berlin of the twenties to a totally different situation.

Brecht was born in 1898, a little after the halfway mark between 1871, when Bismarck finished molding most of the semi-feudal principalities and kingdoms of German-speaking Central Europe into one state, and 1918, when that state began to disintegrate. With nationhood came a belated industrial puberty. German traditions—diligence to duty, bureaucratic organization, an elaborate system of social caste—seemed ready-made for empire; the new middle classes of the day proved the most arrogant of snobs, the most officious of paper-shufflers. It was the age of gunboat diplomacy, of officers who wore spiked helmets and gilt epaulets while they fired the imaginations of meaner men with what Hemingway was later to call the obscene and abstract words, before shooing them forward to die.

Young Brecht, born into the well-to-do home of an Augsburg paper-mill director, reacted early to these traditions. While still a Gymnasium schoolboy, during the opening year of the First World War, he handed in a required essay on "The Glory of Dying for the Kaiser and the Fatherland" that precipitated the first of a lifetime of scandals. For in it he wrote, "The expression that it would be sweet and worthy of respect to die for the fatherland can only be evaluated as purposeful propaganda. . . . Only simpletons can push pride so far as to speak of an easy leap through the dark gateway, and even this only so long as they believe themselves far from the final hour." Such heresies provoked a predictable civic furor, but family influence saved the iconoclast for the time being. Brecht received his diploma, began to study medicine, and then, after his first several terms, was called up to serve as an orderly in a military hospital.

This gave Brecht his first long, close look at the men in the ranks of his society, and after months of bandaging exposed brains in cracked skulls and giving transfusions and amputating limbs and pulling sheets over bloodless faces, he came away with the conviction that war was premeditated butchery and that the social class he grew up in did the planning. In one of his lyric poems he later wrote:

> *I grew up as the son*
> *Of well-to-do people. My parents put a collar*
> *On me and raised me*
> *To be accustomed to being served*
> *And instructed in the art of issuing orders. But*
> *When I was grown and looked around me,*
> *The people of my class did not please me—*
> *Neither giving orders nor being served.*
> *And I abandoned my class and allied myself*
> *With the humble people.*

* See the article "Where there is Total Involvement" by Robert Hatch, in HORIZON for March, 1962.

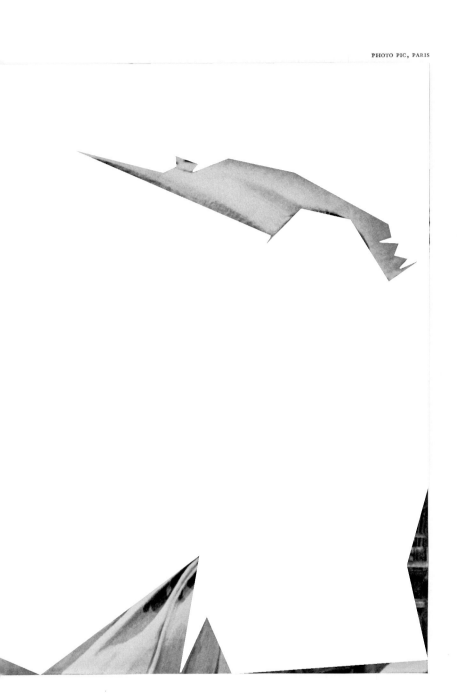

The foremost exponent of Brecht roles is Helene Weigel, his widow and star of the Berliner Ensemble, the troupe he formed in East Germany in the late 1940's. Here she appears as the heroine of Mother Courage, *one of the best known and most widely performed of his works.* Mother Courage *dominates the play and is a sympathetic character, though she sells goods to competing armies and brings about the deaths of her own children.*

At war's end, Brecht returned to the study of medicine. But he had seen too much, and he soon began a subsidiary existence as one of the prime characters of the Munich artistic underworld, as a critic for socialist papers, and as a fledgling dramatist. By 1921 he had given up his medical ambitions, and the people of Munich were beginning to talk about the short, bony, wiry young man with the steel-rimmed glasses, the two days' growth of beard, the hair combed carefully down over his forehead, and the laborer's smock, who spent his evenings in the cellars of Schwabing cabarets croaking vitriolic ballads at his followers.

In 1924, almost at the outset of Brecht's serious career, the astute and prophetic German critic Herbert Ihering came down to Munich from Berlin to see a performance of Brecht's version of Marlowe's *Life of Edward II of England*. "The success of *Edward II*," Ihering reported, "is— like that of *Drums in the Night* [Brecht's earlier play]—the success of an experiencing of our times. Not so much with respect to the actualities, but rather in the sense that he recognizes the anonymous public passions." The culminating phrase is perfect. It seemed to Brecht—it seemed to many Germans during those years—that Germany's stuffy official aims and attitudes and repressions had no right to claim even pragmatic success: the war had been lost; the currency was debased and worthless; the regimes kept on collapsing. Through it all, what was left of the self-righteous, phlegmatic middle class sat placidly on its property, Germany, amiably digesting the political parties one after the other. In the background lay a setting that Brecht projected theatrically to America and particularly to Chicago, in the images of such plays as *St. Joan of the Stockyards*—the lush, phosphorescent jungle city through which pathetic human animals slink, quickly degenerating, goaded by genital hungers and visceral fears.

To express the situation on a stage was not enough for Brecht. Something specific—political—had to be done. Despite his lifelong conviction that truth is concrete, he shared the German weakness for abstraction. Along with many of his generation Brecht became first a pacifist, then a Marxist, and ultimately—although it seems he never officially joined the Party—a professed Communist. By the end of the twenties in Germany the Communists seemed to Brecht and many others the one political group with humanitarian ideals, however distant their realization, that had not sold out to the old order and the industrial and financial barons. Nazism was gathering force, and Brecht, always primarily an intuitive personality, discerned readily the dark threat of the national character and began to grow very frightened by it.

Once aligned with the Communists, Brecht became—or, rather, imagined himself to have become—the most desperate of revolutionaries. Sporting a leather necktie and grimy, visored slouch cap, Brecht affected a cryptic air, a casual toughness, to mask his human susceptibilities. Bent on survival, and convinced that only the cunning survive long, he became a virtuoso of guile: his skill at conversational finesses, evasions, the sliest of double-entendres, and apparent retractions of opinion squeaked him past a lifelong succession of authorities, each hopeful of separating him from his principles or at least finding out what they were. In 1932, for instance, when the Weimar Republic's censor was about to strike down Brecht's Communist-inspired film *Kühle Wampe* on the ground that it dealt with types and not with people, Brecht turned up to defend it. "I stuck strictly to the untruth," he later remarked. "I quoted the individual benefits we had given our unemployed; for example, that one man had put away his wrist watch before jumping out of the window. . . ." The film passed.

As Brecht's political attitude took shape, so did his style. The rhetoric of the earliest plays, with their heroes heaving and sighing over the loneliness of the individual spirit, gave way to a new stage language that was terse, ironic, specific, and brutal. An unashamed borrower all his life, Brecht picked his spare prose rhythms out of the Martin Luther Bible. He learned to set a coarse idea in Swabian gutturals, so that the sounds of the words underscored their meanings. This song from his *Threepenny Novel,* a lengthened version of *Threepenny Opera,* typifies his style:

> *Those people, to whom duty means so much,*
> *Who keep their thoughts on higher goals secure—*
> *The sentiments one learns from literature—*
> *Honorable people are concerned with such.*
> *And so they proudly break the dried-out bread*
> *They earned in honesty: and still they sweat!*
>
> *(Die Leute, die nur ihren Pflichten leben*
> *Und ihren Sinn auf höh're Ziele richten—*
> *Gefühle, die man kennt aus den Gedichten—*
> *Die guten Leute treffen sehr daneben.*
> *Da brechen sie mit Stolz ihr trocknes Brot*
> *Ehrlich verdient; sie sind ganz schweissbedeckt!)*

Brecht advised audiences, in the prologue to *The Exception and the Rule,* to study even the smallest, apparently most simple activities in life, to view them with mistrust, and to question whether they had to be performed as they *were* performed. The problems of external discipline and the submission of the individual to it began to preoccupy Brecht; between 1928 and 1932 he wrote a string of plays intended to inculcate Communist ideas into both actors and audience, starting with *The Flight of the Lindberghs,* including the most "didactic" plays, such as *He Who Says Yes—* and, slyly enough, when the leftist press censured it, *He Who Says No*—and culminating in *The Measures Taken* and a free translation of Gorky's *The Mother*. Of these probably the best was *The Measures Taken.* Composed in the form of a cantata, it deals with the misadventures of a young revolutionary whose warm heart prompts him, while operating as an agent of Moscow, to flout Moscow's orders and assist the coolies, attack a policeman, and lead a premature uprising—for all of which—and at his own request—he is shot.

This was probably the first of Brecht's plays in which his intellectual intentions worked almost at cross-purposes with his imaginative sympathies. The editors of the Berlin Communist press panned his play as being petty-bourgeois and

Brecht always played the true Communist, even in his later years when his sly ridicule of authority bewildered the commissars of the East German regime. His adaptation of Gorky's The Mother *is a party-line document, however, dealing with a middle-aged woman in the city of Tver, in 1917, who becomes a fervent revolutionary only after the Czar's men kill her son. The play has been performed in Paris and in other West European cities.*

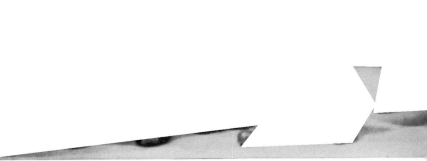

intellectualist. They were much happier with Brecht's contemporaneous *St. Joan of the Stockyards* and its more conventional capitalist target, Pierpont Mauler, the Chicago canned-meat king. Brecht, it was felt, had better leave the thinking to the Party's official thinkers.

Brecht couldn't have agreed less. At the same time that he arrogated to himself the right to comment on Communist political methods, he felt it his duty to create a critical Communist theatre. "I am," he commented, "the Einstein of the new stage form." Brecht tinkered with this new form, to which he soon referred as "epic theatre," for the rest of his life. He built into it everything he thought he could use— from the mechanical steel stage of his early collaborator Erwin Piscator to the pantomime timing of Charlie Chaplin. And it worked.

Epic theatre's basic acting tone and rational calm seem to have been prompted by rebellion and, in particular, rebellion against caste presumption. Anyone who has listened to German officials or actors or orators—especially Nazi orators —is likely to be struck by the outraged tone, the bellow of the superior, the *Obrigkeit* of the martinet, which pervades the speech. Certain critical words seem to fascinate, terrorize, and arouse German audiences, to prepare them for the kinetic words of release—*soil, our folk, iron, might, fight our way out*—by means of which the populace can be provoked to mindless violence and then left so emotionally depleted as to be incapable of resisting new commands.

This process of emotional depletion also occurs in the drama as defined by Aristotle: the spectator is drawn into the tragic dilemma of the actor; he comes to accept the reality of the actor's situation and at first feels pity at the actor's plight, and then terror—as he begins to identify his own personality with the one presented by the actor. Ultimately, as the drama reaches its excruciating resolution, the spectator experiences a total empathy and leaves the theatre purged by the catharsis of his experience. And this "cleaning-out" of all the spectator's stale slag of feeling

was, Aristotle maintained, socially good. Brecht said it was socially bad.

It is not very hard, given Brecht's experiences and personality, to see why. If "Aristotelian" drama burned an audience's social feelings away, the practical effect of this drama would be detrimental. What society in general—and the Communist movement in particular—would have to develop was a theory and practice of the theatre which would describe the conditions of life of a whole group of people, not of an individual. To do this, the dramatist must insure that no one performer becomes the conduit of the spectator's empathy. Brecht therefore began to contrive an elaborate complex of stage techniques to produce the celebrated *Verfremdungseffekt* (the V, or alienation, effect), which could stir audiences without exhausting them. He employed many varieties of the "play within a play" convention to keep the narration detached and avoid "involving" the audience emotionally. He experimented with choruses. He prefaced many scenes with placards or lantern slides that gave away the plotting of the scene to come before suspense could draw people into it. Wherever he could, Brecht exposed the naked wiring, the footlights, the stage flats, the treadmills, or the turntables he was using: this was a *stage*, he insisted, not life, and you had better be aware of that all the time.

He was a master of emphasis. Like Chaplin, whom he admired extravagantly, Brecht would begin with an inherently dramatic situation and so exaggerate the responses of his characters that the whole passage gradually became ridiculous. During a crisis of pathos or of tenderness he was likely to bring on a pair of lunatic, ditty-singing musicians, or allow his mistreated peasant maid of a heroine, with a broad wink at the audience, to make a thoroughly lewd remark about the hero in a *sotto-voce* aside. The situation must not settle. He insisted: "The spectator of the epic theatre says: I wouldn't have expected that—One must not do things that way—That is most striking, almost unbelievable—That must stop—The suffering of this person shakes me because

The setting (left) is English, the language German, the cast Czech, and the work is The Threepenny Opera, Brecht's rollicking variation on Gay's Beggars' Opera. In this 1934 Prague production Tiger Brown (far left) wants Macheath (right) arrested; the beggar king Peachum (below) wants Mack hanged; and Mack wants out.

New York's Living Theatre has lately revived In the Jungle of Cities (opposite), Brecht's contest, placed in an unlikely Midwestern setting, between a wily Malayan lumber dealer and an American innocent. Brecht advised viewers not to look for motives, only to try to "judge the fighting form of the contenders without prejudice."

there is still a solution for him—That is great art: nothing may be assumed—I laugh about those who weep, I weep about those who laugh." Thus the brain, not the emotions, is engaged.

The most influential technique for achieving the V-effect was the style of acting on which Brecht insisted. He militantly rejected the precepts of Stanislavsky, which required that the actor understand and imitate the character being portrayed so that for all dramatic purposes he will *be* the character. The only justification for the actor's effort to "feel his way into the character," according to Brecht, was so that he could ultimately come out "the other side" and observe the character from the standpoint of a seasoned social critic who could add *his own* explicit criticism to his version of the character. In practice this meant that the actor would portray a representative character of the *Lumpenproletariat* as both raw and seriously sympathetic, or a bourgeois, however superficially graceful or powerful, as an ethical cipher. By means of such figures as the alcoholic Mr. Puntila, Brecht drove home his dramatic point: You, the owners, are the truly brutish ones, runs the line of ironic implication; we slaves have remained human. Caught between what he expected and what he actually saw and felt, the cultivated German spectator found himself animated by chronic shock and unwilling recognition. This double view of the characters, this critical supernimbus, would form a true and objective image on the psychological retina of the spectator.

In January of 1933 the Nazis came to power in Germany. When on February 27 a fire broke out in the Reichstag building, the Government seized on the incident as a pretext for rounding up the significant left-wing opposition. The next day, without apology, Brecht fled the country. It was more than just a change of address for Brecht: without a theatre at his disposal, he was like a cello player without his cello. Abruptly, Brecht's first career had come to an end.

For as long as he dared, Brecht kept close to the perimeters of the German-speaking world. After some months in Vienna, Brecht, who had to scrape hard for money throughout the years of his exile, moved his family to a cottage in Denmark. From 1933 to 1939 Brecht, his wife (the actress Helene Weigel), and his two small children waited impatiently in Denmark for the Nazi regime to collapse. He did what he could in the movement of anti-Nazi émigrés—including the brothers Mann, Stefan Zweig, and Lion Feuchtwanger—that disputed the Nazi Government's claim to speak for all Germans. He dabbled in the Danish theatre. He edited an antifascist review, *Das Wort,* published in Moscow. He wrote much good poetry, a ballet, one extremely bad film script, and several conventional, leftist-polemic plays. The critics received these works variously, but the financial returns were standard—poor. Nazi territorial expansion forced Brecht to relocate, first in Sweden, then in Finland, and eventually, when he decided that the Nazis were going to get more before they lost all, in Santa Monica, California.

To imagine how glum and frustrating Brecht found his years in the United States, one must contrast them with the highest of the high old days in Berlin. Lotte Lenya, who, as the wife of Brecht's composer-partner, Kurt Weill, had known him well during the middle twenties, later recollected: "Brecht lived at that time in an attic studio with a skylight, near the intersection Am Knie—no rugs and no curtains to speak of, big iron stove to battle the drafts, typewriter on a massive table, easel on which there stood drawings of costumes and sets, huge couch against the wall. On this couch and around the wall lounged the ever-present disciples, male and female: the men with hair cropped and wearing turtleneck sweaters and slacks; the women without make-up, their hair skinned back, and wearing sweaters and skirts—this highly stylized proletarian style set by the master. Brecht stood alone, looking frail in those days, striding back and forth in a fetid blue cloud from his stogie, pausing for a quick question to this sitter, a snap reaction to a line from another; deep-set brown eyes forever blinking, small white hands continuously gesturing, translating everything in

terms of theatre. Sometimes soundless laughter would shake him, and he would slap his leg in an endearing way until the laughter ended in exhausting pants, leaving him to rub his eyes with the back of his hand and repeat, 'Ja, das Leben. . . .' "

In California "the master" found himself for the most part without pupils. Brecht's denim garb and stubble and nickel cigar meant very little in Hollywood: eccentricity was the rule, and everybody was a figure of social protest. Brecht's English remained stubbornly rudimentary. He made few social contacts outside the Santa Monica community of German intellectual and artistic refugees, and in that community Brecht's reputation was very small beside that of, say, Thomas Mann. He wrote movie scripts and tried to sell them but, except for his scenario for *Hangmen Also Die,* Brecht sold nothing. He seems persistently to have missed the fact that a great many of the ideas he depended on to astound and titillate his German audiences—the moral superiority of the downtrodden, for example, or the corruptibility of authority—were the clichés of the American dream. Much of the time Brecht wavered between being morose and elaborately sceptical.

But gradually, despite his proclaimed uninterest in almost everything American, Brecht attracted attention. Little magazines and the German-language press in New York began to print his poetry. *The Private Life of the Master Race,* the first of Brecht's plays to be produced in New York since the outbreak of the war, failed spectacularly in 1945. And then—most signal of turnings—Charles Laughton helped Brecht translate his play *Galileo* and brought it, with himself in the title role, first to the professional stage in Hollywood and then for a short time to New York.

Commercially, Laughton's *Galileo,* like all of the Brecht plays that had been brought to the American stage, amounted to little. Culturally, it was an event—the first presentation in the United States of one of those plays written between 1933 and 1948 which together constitute the canon of Brecht's mature achievement. The finest of these are, perhaps, *Mother Courage and Her Children, Galileo, The Good Woman of Setzuan, Schweik in the Second World War,* and *The Caucasian Chalk Circle.* The first three were performed during the war in the Schauspielhaus in Zurich; their overwhelming success anticipated their becoming classics of the contemporary German stage.

By late 1947 Brecht was ready to go home. The feeling that had induced him, years before, to take out his first United States citizenship papers had died away with the last of the wartime Soviet-American cordiality. Picked out early as one of the most vociferous Marxists in the motion-picture colony, Brecht spent several of his final hours in the United States double-talking around the questions put to him by the members of the House Committee on Un-American Activities. Ever the master of the soft answer that turneth away the facts, Brecht presented himself to the Congressmen as most willing but insufferably addled. He persistently confused the plot-lines of his various plays. When queried as to whether he had based his writings principally on the doctrines of Lenin and Marx—as he had—he admitted that "as a playwright who wrote historical plays" he had, of course, "studied them." When confronted with his own lyrics from an American Communist songbook and asked whether he had written them, he replied, not without indignation, that he most certainly had not. He had indeed written "a German poem, but that is very different from this." More than placated, the chairman commended him for his good example and closed the proceedings.

Brecht went directly to Switzerland, where his reputation seemed to be reviving, and when the regime in East Berlin offered him a theatre of his own and a subsidy to maintain it, Brecht—after characteristically insuring his personal survival by procuring an Austrian passport, opening a Swiss bank account, and signing a contract with a West German publisher—decided to accept. It was the greatest opportunity of Brecht's life; almost at once, through the unparalleled repertory productions of the Berliner Ensemble, he proved how ready he was to take it.

He spent the last eight years of his life producing, not the Marxian allegories and Communist broadsides of his youth, but the plays he had written in exile. He did not write anything specifically *anti*-Communist or *pro*-Western or religious, even during the later years in Berlin; rather, an intrinsic humanism had gradually moved to the center of his work, infiltrating the materialism of his earlier years.

He showed himself increasingly aware of the mystical, self-contradictory, and inherently tragic sources of the human personality. All his life Brecht had admired certain ideals of the Orient; whenever he had the chance to settle for a time and take up his work, he would unroll and hang beside his desk a painted image of a Confucian elder: this image incarnated for Brecht a society of artful graciousness, of mildness, and of ritualistic courtesy. Before he died, Brecht knew that any code is a disciplined response to a common dilemma. Brecht's Good Woman of Setzuan, Shen Te, laments finally to the perambulating gods:

Your earlier order
To be good and still to live
Split me in halves just like a bolt of lightning. I
Don't know why: to help others
And myself at the same time was something I could not manage.
To help others while helping myself was too hard for me.
Ah, your world is difficult! Too much need, too much despair!
Extend a hand to the sufferer
And he will instantly wrench it out. He who helps the abandoned
Is himself then abandoned!

And the intellectual Galileo Galilei, as Brecht gives him to us, was a man who "treasured the comforts of the flesh. I have no patience with those cowardly souls," Galileo insists, "who speak of its weaknesses. I say: pleasure is an achievement." Brusque, self-centered, sloppy, surpassingly gifted, at once naïve and cynical—a personality cut unmistakably along the lines of Brecht's own—Galileo appears first in Venice, as an impoverished physicist, and manages to insinuate himself into the entourage of the patron of Florence, Cosimo de Medici, and take his chosen place among the fleshpots. Before long he begins to arrive at the conclusions about dynamics that were to destroy the sanctified Ptolemaic world view of physics. Inevitably, the Inquisitor appears and invites the old sybarite to come in for a session with the "instruments"; inevitably, Galileo, unburdened of his assumption that people will believe whatever can reasonably be demonstrated, recants. Truth, he cannot help but agree, is what accords with the system. The rest of the play records Galileo's deterioration as a rationalist and the improvement of his appetites.

Similar themes pervade Brecht's later work. In the parable world of *The Caucasian Chalk Circle* the armored soldiers incessantly switch allegiances, but their single activity, grinding the poor, never varies. Whom was Brecht trying to implicate *here*, the East German authorities were always demanding. What social clique was he epitomizing *there*? Brecht spent much of his last few years explaining and rewriting, but one ambiguity seemed to replace another, and the ironies of the *Verfremdungseffekt* retained their suspicious, double-toned resonances. His concerns now exceeded those of the Communists, his sense of the human predicament became sharp and tragic. At the height of his second career Brecht had developed from a local rebel into a figure of international significance.

In the end, his suspicions must have grown into full fears. The hypocrisies and abuses of the old class order had been superseded by new ones that Brecht was in only too good a position to observe. The new authorities had no hesitation, during the revolt of June 17, 1953, in lifting the one supporting statement from a long, critical letter Brecht wrote to Walter Ulbricht, the chief of the East German regime,

and citing it out of context to prove that legitimate intellectuals were willing to back the regime against the insurgent workers. Among Brecht's literary remains was found a bitter little poem in which, after referring to the regime's solemn admonition that the people could win back the trust of the Government only by redoubled exertion, he suggested poisonously that the Government dissolve the people and elect another.

Something in Brecht had burned out; something else was still glowing. Several days after the pomposity of Brecht's enormous State funeral, the old atheist's last confidant—a Protestant clergyman—published his reminiscences of the conversation. He must write, Brecht had insisted, a candid obituary: "Don't write that you admire me! Write that I was an uncomfortable person, and that I intend to remain so after my death. Even then there are certain possibilities."

If Brecht was prickly, and if his work was pricklier yet, it was because the world as he knew it nettled him so. He meant his writing, his manner, and his "possibilities" to help prod our stolid and unhappy time toward a day when people would know that:

> To let no one be ruined
> Not even yourself
> To fill others with happiness
> Even yourself
> Is good.

Burton Hersh has seen many of Brecht's plays performed on both sides of the Iron Curtain since he first went to Germany as a Fulbright scholar in 1955. He is now a free-lance writer.

Galileo, *another play of the Berliner Ensemble, is Brecht's dramatization of the plight of a scientist who, compelled to suppress his discoveries, lives on to make moral ones at least as prophetic.*

PHOTO PIC, PARIS

THE
OLD WORLD'S
PECULIAR
INSTITUTION

The Greeks and Romans

practiced slavery and condoned it—for war,

for luxury, and for business—

but even then they knew it to be evil

By M. I. FINLEY

A stele celebrates an ancient slave trader

Aulus Kapreilius Timotheus does not appear in any history book. There is no reason why he should, but an accident of archaeology makes him a figure of some curiosity if not importance. He was a slave in the first century of our era who obtained his freedom and turned to slave dealing, an occupation in which he prospered enough to have an expensive, finely decorated marble tombstone seven feet high (see photograph above). The stone was found about twenty years ago at the site of the ancient Greek city of Amphipolis on the Strymon River, sixty-odd miles east of Salonika on the road to the Turkish border—and nothing like it exists on any other surviving Greek or Roman tombstone, though by now their number must be a hundred thousand or more. The stone has three sculptured panels: a typical funeral banquet scene at the top, a work scene in the middle, and a third showing eight slaves chained together at the neck, being led along in a file, accompanied by two women and two children who are not chained and preceded by a man who is obviously in charge, perhaps Timotheus himself for all we know. The inscription in Greek reads simply: "Aulus Kapreilius Timotheus, freedman of Aulus, slave trader."

It is not his occupation that makes Timotheus a rare figure, but his publicly expressed pride in it. The ancient world was not altogether unlike the southern United States in this respect. After the Civil War a southern judge wrote: "In the South the calling of a slave trader was always hateful, odious, even among the slaveholders themselves. This is curious, but it is so." More than two thousand years earlier a character in Xenophon's *Symposium* said to Socrates: "It

is poverty that compels some to steal, others to burgle, and others to become slavers." In neither case was the moral judgment quite so simple or so universally accepted as these statements might seem to suggest, nor was it carried to any practical conclusion, for the most respectable people depended on these same "hateful" men to provide them with the slaves without whom they could not imagine a civilized existence to be possible.

Yet contempt of the slaver was not uncommon, and this suggests that slavery itself was a little problematical, morally, even when it was taken most for granted. On this score ancient and modern slavery cannot be wholly equated. There were special circumstances in the southern states, pulling in contradictory directions. On one hand slavery was "*the* peculiar institution" and few southerners could have been unaware of the fact that most of the civilized world had abolished the practice and did not like it; whereas Greeks and Romans had no such external voice of conscience to contend with. On the other hand southern slaveowners found comfort in the racial factor and in its concomitant, the belief in the natural inferiority of black men—a defense mechanism of which the ancients could make relatively little use. The Negro in the old South could never lose the stigma of slavery, not even when, as an exception, he was freed nor, as was often the case, when he had some white ancestry. But the descendants of an Aulus Kapreilius Timotheus could become ordinary free inhabitants of the Roman Empire, wholly indistinguishable from millions of others.

We have no clue to Timotheus's nationality. His first two

A minor stylized figure of sixth-century B.C. design, this slave crouches on the east pediment of the Siphnian Treasury, built at Delphi to house tribute to the oracle there.

names, Aulus Kapreilius, were those of his master, which he took upon receiving his freedom, according to the regular Roman practice. Timotheus was his name as a slave—a common Greek name that tells us nothing about him, since slaves rarely bore their "own" names but those given them by their masters. In more primitive times the Romans usually called their slaves Marcipor and Lucipor and the like —that is, "Marcus's boy" or "Lucius's boy"—but soon they became too numerous and required individual names so that Marcus's slaves could be distinguished from one another. When that happened there was no limit to the possibilities. The choice was a matter of fashion or of personal whim, though one rough rule of thumb was applied with some consistency. As Roman power spread to the east, the Empire was divided into a Greek-speaking half and a Latin-speaking half, and the naming of slaves tended to follow this division. It is more likely therefore that Timotheus came from the lower Danube, or the south Russian steppes, or perhaps the highlands of eastern Anatolia, than from Germany or North Africa.

To a buyer this question of nationality was important. It was generally believed that some nationalities made better slaves than others, temperamentally and vocationally. Prices varied accordingly, and Roman law (and probably Greek law, too) required the seller to state his chattel's origin specifically and accurately.

One example is worth looking at. In the year A.D. 151 a Greek from Alexandria purchased a girl in the market in Side, a city on the south coast of Anatolia (about two hun-

dred miles west of Tarsus) that had a long tradition and notoriety as a center of slaving activity. He took the girl back to Egypt with him, and also the bill of sale—a bilingual document in Greek and Latin, written on papyrus, which was found in legible condition at the end of the nineteenth century. The girl is described in this way: "Sambatis, changed to Athenais, or by whatever other name she may be called, by nationality a Phrygian, about twelve years of age . . . in good health as required by ordinance, not subject to any legal charge, neither a wanderer nor a fugitive, free from the sacred disease [epilepsy]." The seller guaranteed all this under oath to the gods Hermes and Hephaestus, and under penalty of returning the price twice over should any of it be untrue. The phrase "or by whatever other name she may be called" is a typical lawyer's escape clause; in fact, the girl was born free and given a good Phrygian name, Sambatis, which was replaced by the Greek name Athenais when she was enslaved. How this happened cannot be determined, but it was well known in antiquity that Phrygians often sold their own children into captivity, a practice they continued even after Phrygia was incorporated into the Roman Empire. It is also not stated whether the buyer and seller were professional slave dealers, but Side was a long way to come from Egypt merely to purchase one little girl for oneself.

Bills of sale were usually written on perishable material, so that it is only by accident that a handful, written on papyrus or wax tablets, has survived. This is a pity, because there is no other evidence from which to build a statistical

The Romans, whose military monuments often depict enslaved captives, were quick to turn a profit from their prisoners-of-war. The chained Gaul (left) appears on an arch built at Carpentras, France, about 15 B.C. A detail from the column of Marcus Aurelius (right) shows prisoners and cattle from Germany on their way to market, and in a scene from the Arch of Septimus Severus (far right) a Roman soldier has seized his prize, no doubt during the campaigns in Asia minor, A.D. 194–197. The slave badge (right, above) is a token of less rigorous times: in the fourth century A.D. such metal tags replaced branding as a means of identification. It reads: "Hold me lest I escape, and return me to my master Viventius on the estate of Callistus."

picture of the racial and national composition of the large slave populations of the ancient world. But the broad contours of the picture are clear enough, and they shifted with the times. The crucial point was that there were no specifically slave races or nationalities. Literally anyone and everyone might be enslaved, and which groups predominated at one time or another depended on politics and war. Greeks enslaved Greeks when they could, Romans enslaved Greeks, and they both enslaved anyone else they could lay their hands on by capture or trade.

The majority of slaves, however, were always "uncivilized" from the point of view of the Greeks and Romans. Inevitably the attempt was made, therefore, to justify slavery as an institution on the ground of the natural inferiority of the slaves. The attempt failed: it had to for several reasons. In the first place, there was too large a minority that could not be squeezed into the theory. For example, after the Romans defeated the Carthaginians under Hannibal, they turned east and conquered the Greek world, bringing back to Italy in the course of the next two centuries hundreds of thousands of captives. Among the effects of this involuntary Greek invasion was a cultural revolution. "Captive Greece made captive her rude conqueror," said the Roman poet Horace, and it was manifestly impossible to maintain the doctrine of natural inferiority (which might do for Gauls or Germans) against a people who provided the bulk of the teachers and who introduced philosophy and the drama and the best sculpture and architecture into a society whose virtues had not previously lain in those directions.

In the second place, it was a common practice in antiquity to free one's slaves as a reward for faithful service, most often, perhaps, on one's deathbed. There were no rules about this, but some idea of the proportions that were sometimes reached can be gathered from one of the laws passed by the first of the Roman emperors, Augustus. He tried to put a brake on deathbed manumissions, probably to protect the interest of the heirs, and so he established maxima on a sliding scale, according to which no one man was allowed to free more than one hundred slaves in his will. After centuries of continuing manumission, who could distinguish the "naturally superior" from the "naturally inferior" among the inhabitants of Greek and Roman cities (especially in the absence of any distinction in skin color)?

Human nature being what it is, many individual slave-owners no doubt went right on wrapping themselves in their preordained superiority. But as an ideology the notion was abandoned, and in its place there developed one of the most remarkable contradictions in all history. "Slavery," wrote the Roman jurist Florentinus, "is an institution of the law of all nations whereby someone is subject to another *contrary to nature*." That definition became official: we find it enshrined in the great codification of the law by the emperor Justinian, a Christian emperor, early in the sixth century. Yet no one, at least no one of consequence, drew the seemingly obvious conclusion that what was contrary to nature was wrong and ought to be abolished.

War was the key to the whole operation. The ancient

world was one of unceasing warfare, and the accepted rule was that the victor had absolute rights over the persons and property of his captives, without distinction between soldiers and civilians. This right was not always exercised in full measure; sometimes tactical considerations or pure magnanimity intervened, and sometimes more money could be raised by ransom than by sale into slavery. But the decision was the victor's alone, and a graph would show no more than occasional downward dips in the curve, never a long period (say fifty years) in which fairly large numbers of captives were not thrown onto the slave market. No total figures are available, but there can be no doubt that in the thousand years between 600 B.C. and A.D. 400, the Greeks and Romans between them disposed of several million men, women, and children in this way.

This is not to say that wars were normally undertaken simply as slave raids, though some surely were—as when Alexander the Great's father, King Philip II of Macedon, deliberately undertook an expedition into the Scythian regions north of the Black Sea in order to replenish his depleted treasury in 339 B.C. He is said to have brought back 20,000 women and children along with much other wealth. Granted that this was not a typical affair and that wars usually had other causes, it remains true that the prospect of booty, among which slaves bulked large, was never absent from the calculations—partly to help maintain the army in the field, always a difficult problem in antiquity, but chiefly to enrich both the state and the individual commanders and soldiers. Caesar went off to Gaul an impoverished

nobleman; he died a multimillionaire, and Gallic captives played no small part in bringing about this change of fortune. When he took the town of the Aduatuci, he himself reported that 53,000 were sold off; and after the battle of Alesia in 52 B.C. he gave one captive to each of his legionnaires as booty. Yet Caesar did not plunder to the limit; he often tried conciliatory tactics in the hope of dividing the Gallic tribes, as he did after Alesia when he restored 20,000 captives to the Aedui and Arverni. Half a century earlier, the Roman general Marius, with no reason to be generous to the Germanic Cimbri and Teutones who had penetrated to the south of France, sold all the captives taken at the decisive battle of Arausio (now Orange). The figure we are given on that occasion is 150,000.

That may be an exaggerated number, but human plunder even in quantities only half that size created problems for an army on the march. It could become completely bogged down, and sometimes in fact it was. In 218 B.C. King Philip V of Macedon invaded Elis in the northwestern Peloponnesus and soon found himself so overburdened with booty, which included more than 5,000 captives and masses of cattle, that his army, in the words of the historian Polybius, was rendered "useless for service." He therefore had to change his plans and march through difficult terrain to Heraea in Arcadia, where he was able to auction off the booty.

This case is not typical. If it were, the military and therefore the political history of the ancient world would have been an altogether different one. Normally preparations were made beforehand for booty disposal, and they con-

sisted above all in seeing to it that a crowd of peddlers and merchants came along, equipped with ready cash and means of transport. The booty was assembled at a designated spot and auctioned off (the Spartans, with their characteristic bluntness, gave the responsible officers the title of "booty-sellers"). What happened thereafter was the sole concern of the buyers, and the army was free to continue on its way, enriched by the proceeds.

Possibly the scene on the tombstone of Aulus Kapreilius Timotheus represents just such a situation, the removal on foot of slaves he had bought at an army sale. Certainly this would have been a very profitable business (providing the wherewithal for an expensive marble memorial), for slaves and other booty must have been extremely cheap to buy under such conditions. The only flaw was that war, for all its frequency, was nevertheless irregular and could not guarantee a steady flow of merchandise, and other sources had to be tapped as well. One of these was "piracy," an unfortunate label because it evokes the image of isolated Captain Kidds, whereas the reality was altogether different in scale and character: a continuous, organized activity, illegal yet (like rumrunning) not unwelcome to many of its ultimate beneficiaries, the consumers. Among the Greeks even in classical times this was a traditional occupation in certain areas, especially in the western part of the Greek peninsula.

But that was small stuff compared with the later upsurge in the Roman Republic, beginning about 150 B.C. Then there arose in the eastern Mediterranean a complex business network of pirates, kidnappers, and slave dealers, with its headquarters apparently at Side and its main emporium on the island of Delos (whose docks were rebuilt and extended so that it was possible to turn over as many as 10,000 slaves in a day). The main impetus to this traffic was the rise in Italy and Sicily of the notorious latifundia, large estates or ranches owned by absentee landlords and worked by slave gangs. The profit-side of the trade left a mark on Delos that is still visible today in the excavated remains of the rich houses of the Italian traders.

Direct consequences of the trade were the two greatest slave revolts in antiquity, both in Sicily—the first beginning about 135 B.C., the second a generation later at the same time as the invasion of Gaul by the Cimbri and Teutones. To meet that invasion, Marius was authorized to levy auxiliary troops wherever he could. When he appealed to Nicomedes of Bithynia (along the southwestern shore of the Black Sea), a "client-king" under Roman suzerainty, Nicomedes replied that he had no men to spare because most of his subjects had been carried off into slavery by Roman tax collectors. The Senate was alarmed (by the Germans, not by the complaint) and ordered provincial governors to release any "allied" subjects whom they found in slavery in their districts. Eight hundred were accordingly freed in Sicily, but this was an isolated action that hardly scratched the surface of the problem.

The needs of the latifundia owners were comparatively simple: quantity rather than quality of labor was what they were after. But important as they were, they were not the only consumers. In 54 B.C. Cicero wrote to his friend Atticus

ZERO MOSTEL is a wild-eyed, agile-tongued, broom-mustached actor and comedian with the girth and unpredictable bounce of a football. He is also a painter: not a Sunday dauber or a Pollock-come-lately, but a seriously satirical artist who crams bold, contrasting shapes, lines, and colors onto his semiabstract canvases, many of which command considerable sums of money from collectors.

Mostel is by no means the only theatre and movie celebrity who paints—homemade art hangs in many a living room in Beverly Hills. But he is possibly the only one who has been a professional painter since leaving college and who regards painting not as a hobby or relaxation but as a career. Recently he has been working on a series concerned with the effects of atomic bomb explosions and called "Mutations": tormented, fragmented, red, yellow, and green faces glare out from the walls and easel of his studio; but these are supplemented by lyrical and humorous portraits—*An Old Man Begging*, a box-shaped *Rabbi*, a crowded, transparent subway car on toy wheels.

Mostel was a painter in the Parisian atelier tradition—active but impoverished—from the time he left New York's City College in 1935, when he was twenty, until 1942, when he was persuaded into the entertainment world by a night-club proprietor who had seen him delivering a comic monologue at an artists' ball. Within a year he had moved to an uptown club, La Martinique, and his weekly wage had increased explosively to $3,700.

During his acting career Mostel continued to paint, trying never to let a day go by without putting in several hours at the easel, even after he had progressed to Hollywood (where he played in *The Enforcer, Sirocco, Belvedere Blows the Whistle,* and sundry other films) and to Broadway (where he appeared in, among other shows, *Flight Into Egypt* and Duke Ellington's *Beggar's Holiday*).

In 1958 he won a virtuoso role: that of Leopold Bloom in the off-Broadway production of *Ulysses in Nighttown,* a romping adaptation of several scenes of James Joyce's massive novel about the universe that was Dublin. The performance was truly Mostel in Bloom: skittish, plaintive, acrobatic, deafening—the prancing of an elephant in ballet shoes that might have been lured away from Disney's *Fantasia* by Joyce's blasphemous rhapsody. His next role, perhaps inevitably, was in Eugene Ionesco's comedy *Rhinoceros,* as John, the bellowing best friend of the hero. It was this role that established Mostel as a "marquee name" on Broadway, and from it he went into the lead part in the musical *A Funny Thing Happened on the Way to the Forum.*

As a clown Mostel is a funny fat-man, an Oliver Hardy or Raimu, who improvises off stage in a variety of dialects, ranging from Yiddish to Wodehouse English, and lacing them with what Maxim Gorky, in describing the speech of Tolstoy, called salty peasant words. He specializes in playing the victim of outrageous fortune, set upon by god and man. ("Photographers! What do they know about art? All my life I've been averse to publicity, so I end up my days surrounded by schlemiels who want to take my picture.") At other times, though, Mostel may retreat into silence, even at a party, where one might expect him to play the buffoon.

Mostel's given names are Samuel Joel; he acquired the sobriquet Zero because of ineptitude in elementary school, and this stayed with him through high school and college and his twin careers. He was born into the family of a Brooklyn rabbi forty-seven years ago, and though he is a bulky man, roughly the size of one of the smaller Catskill mountains, he moves with lazy precision and assurance. When I called to see him, he was prone on a day bed in his Manhattan studio, which he redecorated, almost entirely in white, from "a junk heap of a loft." It has been transformed into a combined attic–antique-shop–fun-house by the intrusion of an enormous easel, an outsized table of paints, a couple of hundred expensive-looking art books, clutches of canvases and drawings, neatly collected together and in various stages of completion, a lithograph machine, and hundreds of miscellaneous objects that include a battered top hat, a yellow rocking chair, and a piece of Peruvian pottery.

"Aha, at last—my Boswell," said Mostel, sitting up and putting on a pair of Benjamin-Franklin-style spectacles. "All of a sudden I'm the Jewish Johnson."

He stood up, sat down again on a stool, and began to mix paints, looking strangely like an overgrown kindergartner in finger-painting class. Abruptly, he was on his feet and darting about the studio: he grimaced, crouched, and flew into antic movements while he posed as one celebrated painter after another (see overleaf) and a photographer, enmeshed in trailing wires and equipment, tried desperately to keep up with him. Later he subsided and talked—and his conversation can be astonishingly erudite. An actor who paints professionally is a prodigy; Mostel happens also to be a littérateur who reads Molière in French, can recite long extracts from James Joyce by heart, and closely studies new contributions to the avant-garde theatre.

"For years," he said, "while I was working as a night-club comedian, I really wanted to be an actor, playing roles in the classic comic literature—Shakespeare, Sheridan, Molière, Shaw—but everyone wanted me to be a gagman. In 1949, though, I went up to the Brattle Theatre in Cambridge, Massachusetts, and played Argan in my own adaptation of Molière's *The Imaginary Invalid.* From that time on, people began to realize that I wasn't just another stand-up comic. I've had some bad roles, but lately I've been able to pick and choose. I still hope someday to play Falstaff or Sir Toby Belch, and even to bring Molière to Broadway, leading a repertory company that would do *The Imaginary Invalid, The Doctor in Spite of Himself,* and so forth. As for my art, I have to paint every day or I don't feel alive. Painting is still my first love. I could be uptown running with the Sardi's crowd, but that's not the life I want. I have my family, my career in the theatre, and my easel. The beautiful thing about being a painter is that you can continue to paint all of your life. Eventually every actor is washed up, and even a plumber has finally to give up plumbing, but a painter can go on and on, until the day he dies. And that's what I plan to do—I'll be the goddam Jewish Grandma Moses."

By THOMAS MEEHAN

CONTINUED OVERLEAF

SHARAKU

TOULOUSE-LAUTREC

VAN GOGH

GIOTTO

. . . But
Zero
Is
Many
Men

"If you look at a painting and like it," Zero Mostel observes, "you become it." Here, in a series of swift impressions, Mostel draws on the books and the bric-a-brac in his studio, adds a flick of impudence, and produces eight spoofs of the great artist as a public image. To become Tōshūsai Sharaku, Mostel needs no props other than his head. With a top hat and evasive mien he becomes Lautrec leaving the Folies. Chagall is surmounted by a rooster and clutches a spray of flowers, while Rousseau takes refuge, like some wild animal, behind

CHAGALL

ROUSSEAU

CÉZANNE

PICASSO

a potted plant. A white bandage suggestively conceals the spot where Van Gogh's ear was and also does duty as the sweatcap worn by Cézanne when he was out-of-doors interpreting the landscapes of Provence. One of Giotto's angels is manufactured by means of a heavenward glance of devotion and a gold-rimmed plate, and the fractured, Picasso-like face results from a pair of spectacles on the skew and a tortured mouth. "In painting, as in acting," Mostel explains, "you arrive at the truth through a sense of distortion and exaggeration."

BERNARDA BRYS

A MEMORANDUM

From: Sigmund Freud

To: Norman Mailer, Tennessee Williams, Alberto Moravia, Jean Genet, et al.

Subject: On totally freeing the libido

A little less than sixty years ago, when I published my path-breaking *Three Essays on the Theory of Sexuality,* my investigations into the role of the libido and its repression and sublimation were greeted, as you know, with cries of righteous outrage. Even to the end of my days I was looked upon in certain high-placed quarters as a corrupter of the moral order. How the world has changed, and how are the once-mighty fallen!

What in my prime could hardly be mentioned even in a clinical context is now freely tossed about in almost every well-regarded new novel, play, or film. Not only that, but in many cases it appears to form its very substance. I am informed that there are almost no effective public censors any more, and that liberty increasingly rules *your* moral order. Shall we, then, presume that the day is near when the power of those interior censors that have so long shackled the id drives of modern man will be broken as well? You will recall that in my paper "Civilized Sexual Ethics and Modern Nervousness" (1908) I argued that although the achievements of civilization had been brought about by the suppression of instincts, this process appeared to have gone too far for its own good, since so much sexual constraint was the result. Perhaps I should be the first to congratulate gentlemen like yourselves on being instrumental in reversing man's course and bringing us within so few years to the verge of a millennium that might see an end to most repression, inhibition, and *Angst.*

I observe, though, that in your creation of works of art dealing with sexuality at its freest, you often become absorbed with this topic to the exclusion of anything else. It is almost as if you identified all art with an erogenous zone. I trust you do not base yourself on me in this respect: my own interests, of course, were somewhat more diversified. I also observe, particularly in the books of Mailer, Moravia, and Genet (to whom one could also add H. Miller, W. Styron, the earlier L. Durrell of *The Black Book,* and a host of minor authors) an impulse to describe sexual encounters in minute and indeed exhausting detail, leaving nothing to the imagination. In my own writings, however, I included such details only when they were clinically and therapeutically relevant.

In some of your works, moreover (beginning in fact with those of the late D. H. Lawrence), I find a disconcerting resort to the kind of words one finds scribbled on the walls of public conveniences, as if the authors—who must know other words for the same things—were under some compulsion to use these. I would remind you, if freedom is the issue, that perhaps the freest celebration of sexuality yet published in the English language, the memorable *Fanny Hill,* was written throughout in the most decorous language of its period. I am a little astonished that this classic is still denied a place on booksellers' shelves, when yours are not.

Unlike the author of *Fanny Hill,* however, whose attitude toward sex leaves of no doubt, you, I feel, are often highly ambivalent in yours. Though you dwell on sex continually —I might almost say obsessively—the more you say about it the more you seem to express surfeit, disenchantment, unpleasure. Thus Mailer in his *The Deer Park* and H. Miller in his *Tropic* books often identify erotic scenes with degradation of one or both of the partners. Genet, in his autobiographical *Our Lady of the Flowers,* identifies them with his own degradation. Roger Vadim in his film *Les Liaisons Dangereuses* (widely advertised as extremely naughty) manages to make a carnival of adultery positively dreary. Moravia, in *The Empty Canvas,* describes his characters' multiplying sexual encounters as an escape from boredom, only to conclude that these are boring, too. And the dream-work of Williams throughout his plays seems out to suggest that strong heterosexual activity inevitably leads, like a crime, to punishment (in *Sweet Bird of Youth,* to castration). Though I myself have written in several papers about the castration complex, I trust I never gave rise to any notion such as this. Who, indeed, is Williams's current analyst?

If I were among you today, I think I would say that the result of all this is to arouse in your audiences a certain revulsion against sexuality; and I wonder, gentlemen, whether this has not been your actual though unavowed intention all along. Far from being the wholly liberated and libertarian spirits you would like your fellows to think you are, are you not in fact a new school of Puritans traveling under false colors? You titillate, you scrawl on walls, so to speak, and some of you feel impelled on occasion to shout obscenities (I have seen, clinically, some published work of the recent J. Kerouac and A. Ginsberg, too): but this is a typical manifestation of the Puritan, who does not really free himself by compulsive exhibitions in public. Basically, I believe, your attitude remains anti-sex, and your impulse is to transfer this attitude to your public also. It is you yourselves who are the new restraining super-ego. If the public turns against the extremes of your work and invokes new censorship, it will of course only be playing your own game.

WILLIAM HARLAN HALE

Atop bookcase in Freud's gallery: the spirit of D. H. Lawrence. Next tier, from left: Moravia, William Styron, Genet. Below them, Allen Ginsberg, Lawrence Durrell. Foreground and reflected at top rear: Mailer. From center to right, clockwise, Jack Kerouac, Henry Miller, Roger Vadim, Williams.

Derided now and burdened by its aging dignity,

it was a brilliant, full-blooded force in its prime

THE ROYAL ACADEMY

Before the stately façade of Burlington House, seat of the Royal Academy, stands a statue of its first President, Sir Joshua Reynolds. His self-portrait with a bust of Michelangelo (opposite) was painted in 1773, five years after he took office.

By JOHN RUSSELL

57

Above: Surrounded by new paintings, old silver, and a timeless cross section of the British Establishment, the President of the Royal Academy—Sir Charles Wheeler—begins the traditional round of toasts at the Annual Dinner in 1961. The guests, who have just dined on lobster, chicken, raspberry soufflé, and Old Blue Cheshire, include Prime Minister Macmillan (seen to the left of the President's chair), the Swedish ambassador (next left), and the conductor Sir Malcolm Sargent (at the right, below the portrait). *Right:* In the same room some seven months later, a somewhat different cross section in khakis and tweed jackets (and with more adventurous work on the walls), awaits the annual distribution of prizes by Sir Charles to students of the R.A. schools.

Of all the great private palaces that once stood in Piccadilly and its London neighborhood, Burlington House alone remains intact, unchanged, and in traditional hands. Not that it is "private" in the strict sense, but simply that it has been since 1867, and is due to remain for the next nine hundred and four years, the home of the Royal Academy of Arts, the institution founded in 1768 under George III's patronage in the interests of the living British artist, and now linked in many minds chiefly with the names of the not-so-living and the dead.

Rising behind a forecourt in which a whole regiment of foot soldiers could once have paraded, the splendid quasi-Palladian pile of Burlington House is a pillar of the Establishment and at present the seat of twelve elected Senior Academicians (including Sir Gerald Kelly, K.C.V.O., and Dame Laura Knight, D.B.E.), thirty-seven Academicians (including Louis de Soissons, C.V.O., O.B.E., and the President, Sir Charles Wheeler, K.C.V.O., C.B.E.), two Honorary Retired Academicians, two Honorary Academicians, two Senior Associates, a swarm of just plain Associates, a glittering panel of Honorary Members and Honorary Members Ex-Officio (headed by the retired Archbishop of Canterbury), and one Honorary Academician Extraordinary (The Rt. Hon. Sir Winston S. Churchill, K.G., O.M., F.R.S., M.P.). It possesses an extraordinary collection of "diploma" paintings and memorabilia of Academicians over the generations; it maintains a school, exhibits (and sells) the work of nonmembers as well as of members at its vast Summer Exhibitions; and, above all, it mounts splendid Winter Exhibitions of older works—such as, to look back before the late war, its celebrated shows of Italian, Flemish, Dutch, and Chinese art and, in the years soon afterward, Russian art, Portuguese art, and French works of the Louis XIII and Louis XIV periods.

Yet this same Academy has been derided for generations by all those whose concern is, or was, with new art. J. M. W. Turner was the last great artist to have been nurtured, in any real sense, by the Academy—and Turner died in 1851. When the R.A. has had a chance to prove its judgment in the purchase of work by living artists, the result has been disastrous. And only a few years ago the then President of the R.A. boasted in public of his ambition to give Picasso a running kick from behind. And an artist who was to be one of his successors resigned from the British Arts Council when that body persisted in spending public funds on an exhibition of sculptures by Giacometti. The Academy seems, in fact, to have a double nature: generous, unselfish, and enlightened in its private dealings; erratic and wrong-headed when brought face to face with art as it has developed since (let us say) 1908.

Here it shares in the world-wide decline of all "official" institutions that have to do with the arts. Nobody believes any longer in the existence of immutable laws of art; any institution that sets itself up as the guardian of such laws is, by that very fact, a thing of the past. There is still a tyranny of taste, but the tyrants concerned are dealers and critics and individual collectors and patrons. To be a member of the Royal Academy was once a great advantage—financial, social, and professional—to a young artist; today it is a handicap, on all three counts, to anyone but the full-time portraitist. To the R.A. this is a mortifying and injurious situation, and one from which it would give a good deal to extricate itself; for no longer, as many people suppose, is its face set firmly against the future. There is hardly a single serious artist in Britain who would not be welcome in the R.A. if he chose to present himself for admission. (Not everyone realizes, for that matter, that an artist *must* so present himself—or that an artist cannot be elected to membership in the R.A. against his will.) Sir Jacob Epstein and Matthew Smith—to name two eminent British artists who have recently died—would have been welcome in the R.A. at any time in the past quarter of a century, and so today would many of those who have won international acclaim since the war. The Academy wants (or would accept) them, but they don't want the Academy. To know why this has come to be, one must look back over the R.A.'s history.

When the word "academy" first came into European usage in the mid-fifteenth century it meant not "a school" but "a philosopher's country house." To the humanists of the Italian Renaissance, it meant a place where discussion was informal and free. The university then stood for a pedantic rigidity and the academy, if you were lucky enough to be admitted to one, for the vivacious and privileged intercourse of superior and liberated spirits. (Before long, however, the original notion of academic inquiry became too subversive for general use in a society that was heading for the rigors of the Counter Reformation, and for the ideal freedom of the original groups there was substituted an organization as elaborate as it was tight.)

In the case of most European academies, official patronage and formal constitution were preceded by a decade or more of private activity. Officialdom took over a going concern. This is true, for example, of the founding in 1635, at Richelieu's instigation, of the Académie Française, and it is true also of the founding in 1662 of the Royal Society in London. So brilliant was the history of the Royal Society in its first hundred years, with Newton, Halley, and Sir Christopher Wren in full activity, that it may seem odd that British painters did not get around to forming their own academy till 1768. But the truth is that there were not

enough British artists of consequence to press on with any such idea. And there never had been. Alongside the genius of a Holbein, a Van Dyck, or a Rubens, the British artists of their times were completely outclassed.

But by the middle of the eighteenth century there were artists like Reynolds, Hogarth, Gainsborough, and Richard Wilson who could compare with the best of their contemporaries on the Continent. What was lacking was an instrument for direct negotiation between artists and public—or, for that matter, permanent headquarters where the new dignity of the professional could be reinforced and made visible.

These were the forces behind the formation of the various artists' societies which, in 1768, were metamorphosed into the Royal Academy of Arts. There was a young king (George III, who was thirty that year); there was a public that would pay to see new pictures (profits of the annual show of the Society of Artists grew steadily in the 1760's, and in 1766 amounted to £874, the equivalent of nearly ten thousand of today's dollars); and although the *cognoscenti* were still preoccupied with the supposed superiority of European art, the political situation made it difficult for them to get across the Channel. All that was needed was for somebody of commanding diplomatic gifts to come along and realize what was, however confusedly, already in the air. The person who did this was Sir Joshua Reynolds; and we can judge of the difficulties involved by the fact that in his inaugural discourse he spoke of the "numberless and ineffectual consultations" that had preceded the founding of the R.A. with the King's approval and with himself in the chair as President.

This honor he owed to his outstanding gifts not merely as artist and man of the world but as catalyst and manipulator. No man who was not in himself remarkable could have been the close friend of Johnson, Burke, Goldsmith, and Boswell; and where Johnson was concerned Reynolds had something akin to genius in the imagination and resource of his friendship (Johnson admired, in particular, Reynolds's ability to be "the same one day as another").

Reynolds was forty-five when the R.A. came into being, and he remained its President till he died twenty-four years later. He, more than any other man, gave the institution its tone. That tone was not to everyone's taste. To this day it exasperates those who feel that it is no part of an artist's business to treat with the world of wealth and fashion on its own terms. To this day we can see the corrupting influence of high society on artists who allow themselves to be annexed by it ("Live like a pig and paint like Titian" may be an unwelcome injunction in the days of the affluent society, but to live like Titian and paint like a pig is a still more injurious alternative).

It was William Blake who put the extreme anti-Reynolds case. As a student of the R.A. schools in 1778 he had not been happy, and throughout his life he felt that, as he wrote

Thomas Rowlandson took a satiric view (left) of the comings and goings at the Summer Exhibitions in Somerset House, the R.A.'s home from 1780 to 1836. But an engraving dated 1787 (right) shows that the public was properly subdued in the presence of so many paintings.

in the margins of Reynolds's *Works,* "This Man was Hired to Depress Art." What was important in England, he wrote, "is not whether a Man has Talents & Genius, but whether he is Passive & Polite & a Virtuous Ass & Obedient to Noblemen's Opinions in Art & Science. If he is, he is a Good Man: if not, he must be Starved." Observe the imposing nobodies at an Academy private view today, watch the artist-patron relationship in action, and you will agree that there is still something in what Blake said.

Reynolds, however, believed that the artist was not a gypsy or an itinerant comedian, to come begging at back doors for the chance of showing his skill, but a professional gentleman who should be able to treat with the great figures of this world as prince with prince. For this he needed security and an imposing establishment—but he also needed the kind of personal distinction which not many artists of that day could claim. Reynolds was just the man. "His table," a contemporary wrote, "was frequented by men of the first talents. Politics and party were never introduced. Temporal and spiritual peers, physicians, lawyers, actors and musicians composed the motley group." This tradition is kept up today not only at the Annual Dinner (see photograph, pages 58–59) preceding the opening of the Summer Exhibition but at the occasional dinners given by the President in the Academy's private rooms. One day last year, for instance, readers of the *Times* were informed that on the previous evening the President's guests had included the Duke of Devonshire, Sir Kenneth Clark, Sir Basil Spence (architect of the new Coventry Cathedral), Sir Arthur Bliss (Master of the Queen's Musick), T. S. Eliot, Yehudi Menu-

hin, and Dame Adeline Genée (the pioneer of British ballet).

Conviviality has always played a great part in the life of the Academy: every member is encouraged, for instance, to present a piece of silver for the Academy's table; and when the wine passes round and the platters of plain meats are served by the Academy's lace-collared staff, it is not too difficult to imagine that Goldsmith and Horace Walpole, Boswell and Dr. Johnson, will presently come and join the talk. For it is to Reynolds that the R.A. owes not only its high place in English society but the easy and expansive tone of its entertainments.

Other traditions inaugurated in Reynolds's day are still intact: tuition in the R.A. schools is still free, and there are still traveling scholarships to Italy; funds are available for members, and their dependents, who may have fallen on hard times; and the Academy still lives by its own exertions, entirely independent of public monies. It is connected, even if only ornamentally, with the Church, the Armed Forces, and the worlds of learning and diplomacy. It has a Chaplain (the former Archbishop of Canterbury); a Professor of Ancient History (the Earl of Crawford and Balcarres); a Professor of Law (Viscount Simonds); a Secretary for Foreign Correspondence (the Marquess of Salisbury): all are honorary posts. Earlier holders of one or another of them include Gibbon, Johnson, Goldsmith, Walter Scott, Grote, Macaulay, Gladstone, and Browning; none of them, however, attracted as much public attention as did Sir Anthony Carlisle, the Academy's Professor of Anatomy from 1808 to 1824. A police guard was called out to restrain the crowds whenever Sir Anthony lectured; but what stirred the mob was not so much the academic content of the lectures as the auxiliary matter with which he diversified them. Often, for instance, he would have human remains handed round on dinner plates, the better to make his point; and for a time he illustrated the operation of the muscular system with the help of eight private soldiers of the Foot Guards who exercised stark naked on the lecture platform.

Living artists still can obtain practical advantages within the R.A., though many disdain to make use of them. Their work is shown and sold free of commission, for instance, at the Summer Exhibition, and the R.A. maintains a sales network, discreet but elaborate, on behalf of its members. Altogether, therefore, and in all outward forms, it has a persistent regard for the foundations laid by Sir Joshua.

But those forms are preserved and shored up in a world that has less and less respect for them. As far as the fostering of new art is concerned, the Summer Exhibition has not for many years been the object of serious ambition: the Academy is approaching its bicentenary at a time when showing at the R.A. is a positive handicap to success elsewhere. The social prestige for which Reynolds maneuvered so skillfully is now regarded by many artists as both fatuous and abhorrent, and the international rehabilitation of the British School over the period 1945–1962 is an achievement in which the R.A. has played no part.

The real power of the Academy lay in its early days, and the driving force behind its consolidation was not primarily intellectual or social at all. It related to the machinery of distribution and sale. High thinking and good social connections were all very well; but what really counted, when the Annual Dinner had been eaten and cleared away, was the chance of showing new pictures in grand surroundings and under Royal patronage. There were auctioneers and printsellers in Reynolds's time (in fact the Academy's first show, in 1769, was held in Lambe's Auction Rooms in Pall Mall), but as far as new pictures went the R.A. had a monopoly of large-scale display. It was the artist's natural showroom, and this advantage it retained for more than a century —till 1875, in fact, when the modern art world in London began with the opening of the Grosvenor Gallery.

William Powell Frith, a leading Academician of his day, painted his Private View of the Royal Academy, 1881 *on the subject of its Summer Exhibition of that year and the celebrities who attended it. In his autobiography he said his intention was to satirize "aesthetic" fashions in dress and to comment on "the folly of listening to self-elected critics in matters of taste." By now the satire has evaporated, and what is left is not only an illustration of the Victorian taste for densely populated canvases and meticulously rendered details, but a useful social document. Frith includes the portraits of such prominent taste-makers as Anthony Trollope (far left, with top hat and gray beard), Gladstone (nearer left, bareheaded and clean-shaven), Browning (bareheaded and graybearded), T. H. Huxley (center, brown sideburns and brown suit), and young Oscar Wilde (right center, top hat and lily boutonniere).*

This is the reality behind the great days of the Royal Academy. It could have been said of it in Reynolds's day, as it was said later of the House of Commons, that it was "the best club in London"; its bias was genuinely of a higher-educational sort, but it also owed something of its character to that great English trait, the wish to put a good face upon trade. And the Academy was (and is still) very well run: it was not by swapping quotations from Plotinus on the Sublime that it saved and invested £12,000 in its first decade. Reynolds was a secular Good Shepherd in more ways than one, and it was due to the broad lines of his initial direction that, until 1851, anyone who spoke of "the Exhibition" was automatically understood to mean the Royal Academy's annual show.

But Reynolds could not live forever. His successor, Benjamin West, had a Presidency of twenty-eight years (1792–1820). Unlike Reynolds, whose friendship with Burke was displeasing to the King, he was a favorite with George III,

who had backed him ever since he arrived in London from Pennsylvania in the 1760's. The idea that an American could paint was a great novelty in those days, and it may be that this element of surprise, combined with West's gentle and dignified manners (he came of a family of Quakers), caused his admirers to waive their normal standards of judgment. Certainly it seems odd that Sir Thomas Lawrence should have said of West's work that it was "unexcelled anywhere at any period since the schools of the Carracci."

West's Presidency was a time of great importance for British art in that, on the one hand, Turner, Constable, Lawrence, Flaxman, and Chantrey came to maturity and, on the other, normal intercourse between England and the Continent was very largely suspended by the Napoleonic wars. This suspension resulted in a hot flush of nationalist sentiment. The feeling got about that there was nothing that British artists could not attempt; the Exhibition of 1815 made the enormous sum of £5,255; and there was, in Sir

Thomas Lawrence, an artist equally gifted as painter, connoisseur, and man of the world.

All was not well, however. Many agreed with William Collins, who said, "If it were not for the Academy, artists would be treated like journeymen"; but there was also much in William Hazlitt's forthright assertion that "the R.A. is a mercantile body like any other mercantile body, consisting chiefly of manufacturers of portraits . . . who, with the jealousy natural to such bodies, supported by authority without, and by cabal within, think themselves bound to crush all generous views and liberal principles of Art, lest they should interfere with their monopoly and their privilege to be thought Artists and men of genius." Lawrence, who succeeded West as President, was not the man to put these things right; few artists with so generous a share of the outward graces have paid so heavily for the ability to please. (An entry in Greville's *Memoirs* for January 22, 1830, reads: "Lawrence was buried yesterday. A magnificent fu-

neral, which will cost, they say, £2000. . . . Pretty well for a man who was certainly a rogue and a bankrupt and probably a bugger.") Among the privileges complained of was the opportunity of repainting a picture, on what was called varnishing-day, to give it an advantage over its neighbors on the wall. Hazlitt tells of one "little lively knight of the brush" who submitted a portrait of a lady in a white dress, took note of the tonality of the pictures hung next to it, called for vermilion and Indian yellow, and in half an hour made his portrait stand out "like the drop-curtain at Covent Garden."

Such things distressed an injured minority, but as long as the Academy could assemble the best new pictures of the year in surroundings as splendid as those of Somerset House, its first home in the eighteenth century, most people were well enough pleased. Thomas Rowlandson might make fun of the auxiliary amenities of the "exhibition stare-case" (see page 61), but the public as a whole never tired of the Great Room, 53 by 43 feet, and 32 feet high, in which canvases were hung five and six deep, as if in a gigantic campaign tent, with the upper rows leaning inwards and the whole enormous collection (1,165 pictures in 1821, for instance) interlocked with hardly an inch of wall visible anywhere. The Academy moved into the Victorian age with something very near to the unanimous support of the British public.

In 1837 the Academy moved from Somerset House to rooms that had been provided for it by the Crown in the new National Gallery building in Trafalgar Square. The period that followed was in many ways one of the happiest in the history of the Academy. It had Turner, perhaps the greatest of all British artists, in full output (even if his latest and most adventurous works were taken as evidence of mental decay). It had as its President from 1850 to 1865 Sir Charles Eastlake—no great painter, perhaps, but one of the finest connoisseurs England has ever produced, and a man who, as was once said, "bore the stamp of *gentleman* in the utter absence of all anxiety to show it." The Royal Academy schools nurtured in the 1840's three students who were to create a revolutionary movement in British art: John Millais, Dante Gabriel Rossetti, and Holman Hunt. And when these Pre-Raphaelites sent in their first controversial pictures in 1849 and 1850, they were all prominently hung. One may wonder how many Academies, now or at any other time, would have given such treatment to painters barely out of their teens.

Individual acts of kindness could not, however, change the fact that the Academy's formal constitution, then as now, made it ponderous and slow moving. There were forty full members of the R.A., and till recently their appointment was for life (effective membership now ceases at seventy-five). It is as if new blood were admitted to Congress or Parliament only when a Representative or Member had happened to die: no such assembly could reflect current opinion. In the 1850's and 60's it was taken for granted by younger and livelier artists that the life-membership system empowered those who were inside the R.A. (the words here are Holman Hunt's) "to keep the prestige of the Institution for their own advantage and to delay for years, and sometimes forever, the acceptance of artists of independent power."

Holman Hunt was admittedly an interested witness. But the point here is that it was possible to voice such views and survive: the R.A. was no longer all-powerful. As Hunt said in 1863: "The only national school which has grown up at all, has grown up outside the Academy, and indeed in opposition to it—that is, the water color school; and the only definite reform movement (the Pre-Raphaelite school) was certainly not stimulated by the R.A., and even met with opposition from it."

And yet as a social mechanism the Academy had never run more smoothly. To this period the diaries of Lady Eastlake, wife of the President, are an invaluable guide. She was, in her own right, one of the cleverest women of the day, with a Mary McCarthy's sharpness of tongue and the social versatility of a Freya Stark. Here she is, after the Private View of the Summer Exhibition of 1856:

Yesterday's Private View was very interesting. The Duke and Duchess of Northumberland were there, always polite and kind; dear old Lady Morley rattling away, and Lady Somers more beautiful than anything or anybody else. The account of the pictures in "The Times" is nonsense: in most cases the exact reverse of what they say may be taken as the truth. Paton's picture of a soldier, one-armed, footsore and ragged, returned home and the mixed emotions of wife and mother is *the* picture: few came away from it with dry eyes.

The reverential tone of her allusions to the Duke and Duchess, and her espousal of Paton's anecdote as *the* picture of the year, are symptoms of the insecurity and natural

TEXT CONTINUED ON PAGE 73

THE R.A. IN ITS HEYDAY

A PORTFOLIO IN GRAVURE

For almost a hundred years after its founding in 1768 the Royal Academy was linked with the greatest names in British painting, from Joshua Reynolds to J. M. W. Turner. Representative works by five of them appear in this portfolio. All were full Academicians except George Stubbs, the renowned portrayer of horseflesh, whose election in 1781 was for some reason not ratified, although he continued to exhibit there as an Associate. But Turner was the last; after him, with few exceptions (Augustus John was one), British artists whom we regard as important today made their careers without any encouragement from the R.A.—and in many cases, even if it had been offered to them, they would have spurned it.

64

SIR THOMAS LAWRENCE (1769–1830): "PRINCESS LIEVEN," c. 1820

THOMAS GAINSBOROUGH (1727–1788): "MR. AND MRS. ROBERT ANDREWS," c. 1748

GEORGE STUBBS (1724–1806): "HAMBLETONIAN; RUBBING DOWN," 1800

JOHN CONSTABLE (1776–1837):

"THE LEAPING HORSE," 1825

TEXT CONTINUED FROM PAGE 64

bad taste of the day. It was all very well for Lady Eastlake to say that "the British public has scarcely advanced beyond the lowest step of the aesthetic ladder, the estimate of a subject"; that estimate was, often enough, as far as she herself was willing to go. Eastlake had taught himself Latin and Greek, the better to find subjects for history-painting, and he was one of the finest men who ever sat in the Presidential chair. And yet if we compare him with Turner—his learning and wit and kindness and social resource against Turner's complete unrespectability of speech, dress, bearing, manners, and outlook—there is no doubt as to where original genius lay. Lady Eastlake's visit to Turner is instructive in this connection: even his housekeeper aroused her disfavor ("A hideous woman is such a mistake," she noted). His rooms were even worse—"penury and meanness written on every wall and every article of furniture." And Turner himself, with his reddened and blotchy features, his overlong dress coat, his "not over-clean hands," his rollicking eye, and his "continuous, though, except to himself, unintelligible jokes," was not easy swallowing for the President's wife. But at least she made light of it in a story that is one of the classics of art appreciation: "Seeing a picture in his studio in which all the elements were in uproar I incautiously said, 'The End of the World, Mr. Turner?' To which he replied: 'No, Ma'am—Hannibal Crossing the Alps.'"

In general the notion of the artist as wild man would have been quite out of place in the R.A. in Eastlake's day. It has been customary for a very long time to deplore indiscriminately the general level of the pictures which resulted; and that level is, of course, absurdly low if we consider that across the Channel 1855 was the year of Courbet's "Pavillon du Réalisme" at the World's Fair in Paris, 1862 the year of Manet's La Musique aux Tuileries, and 1866 the year of Monet's Camille. As G. M. Young once wrote: "The notion of art as an enclosed world, obedient to its own laws only, did not come easily to a race which thought of the painter as an upper-class decorator, a recorder of domestic incident, winning landscapes, and right sentiments." An institution which was by its very nature consolidatory could hardly be blamed for reflecting those half-conscious but immensely powerful drives toward security and reassurance that everywhere characterized the mid-Victorian age.

The lessons we learn today from Victorian painting are primarily of a documentary order; and the works in question should perhaps not be considered under the heading of painting at all, but rather as adjuncts and auxiliaries of the Victorian novel. Not surprisingly it is in the city art galleries of Birmingham, Manchester, and Liverpool that the masterworks of high Victorian anecdote abound, for in those great fortresses of industrial society new money was spent by the fistful on work perfectly adapted to current demand. Painters like William Powell Frith, G. E. Hicks, Frank Stone, and Abraham Solomon knew that what people wanted

was to see the life of their own time portrayed with as much as possible of identifiable detail.

The new generation of merchant collectors did not need to go on the Grand Tour to pick up Italian pictures in Venice or Naples: they stayed at home and looked to the Academy for reassurance that their own country and their own day could produce all they needed. The painters of the fifties, sixties, and seventies were not afraid, any more than Dickens was afraid, of sentiments we might now consider uncomfortably obvious and broad. The broken engagement, the landlord's cruel letter, the bank failure, the sailor's return, the doctor's dread message—these were the subjects that an eager public would queue to see. By the end of the seventies, however, the level of pictorial quality was abysmally low. Perusal of Henry Blackburn's illustrated Academy Notes reveals a very high proportion of works too gruesome to be discussed even under the anesthetic of irony. "Refinement and earnestness of purpose" are qualities much acclaimed by Blackburn. "An eloquent sermon, ably expressed" is another favorite encomium; and when he looks for "the picture of the year" in 1876 he picks on Luke Fildes's The Widower: "The sombre interior of a laborer's cottage. Mother dead; father, who has just returned from work, clay-stained and weary, nurses a sick child."

These were times of enormous prosperity for the admired artist. Whereas Turner, for instance, had asked forty to eighty guineas for his very best water colors, the engraving rights alone of Holman Hunt's Christ in the Temple fetched £5,500 in 1860; and Frith, for his Railway Station, got £5,250 in the same year. Painters like Millais and Landseer were as rich as many of their patrons, and when Millais was made a baronet in 1885 the social advancement of the profession seemed to have entered upon a new phase. It is from this period that we may date the large number of elaborate and often phantasmagorical artists' villas still standing in London's Holland Park, West Kensington, and St. John's Wood. Set as a rule in large gardens, where on occasion a zebra or brace of exotic wild fowl could be glimpsed, these often contained architectural elements derived from Nuremberg, Venice, India, and the Far East.

Minarets, a neoclassical pediment, and a miniature Bridge of Sighs would be found on one and the same building. Within, the incongruities could be more startling still. The studio was, naturally enough, the showpiece of the house: with its potted palms, fountains, fragments of stained glass, mosaics, draped throne, and portable organ it was, indeed, a place not soon forgotten. Elsewhere a vast bow window would suggest that the sea, or even Italy's Euganean Hills, might be revealed at daybreak; billiard room and conservatory would remind the Academician in his leisure moments of the ducal households where he was an honored guest in August and September; staircases would be wide enough, and high enough, for a carriage and pair; the wallpaper would look like embossed leather, the auk's egg would be

TEXT CONTINUED ON PAGE 78

73

J. M. W. TURNER (1775-1851): "THE PASSAGE OF THE ST. GOTHARD, FROM THE CENTER OF DEVIL'S BRIDGE," 1804

THE ACADEMY BECOMES ACADEMIC

During the last half of the nineteenth century, when the impressionists were revolutionizing art across the Channel, the Royal Academy gave its imprimatur only to the bland, the sentimental, and the safe. One of the most accomplished painters to exhibit there (though not a member) was James Tissot, who might almost have been a Renoir—except that in art, as in everything else, "almost" covers a wide gap. He was especially good with ships and beautiful women, as his Ball on Shipboard (above) shows. It is thought to represent an actual occasion, perhaps a dance aboard the royal yacht at Cowes in 1873; the double-headed eagles among the flags overhead suggest that the event might have honored Czar Alexander II, although one also notes the Stars and Stripes. What Tissot did, the color camera does today; but his charming, inconsequential picture is infinitely more attractive to us than most of the Diploma Works that were deposited in the R.A. during this period—and long afterward—by newly elected Academicians. These usually fell into a few predictable categories: the coy nude, the high-class cultural nude, the anecdote, the portrait-conversation piece, and the Biblical theme. Examples of each are, opposite, the bronze Elf (top left) by Sir William Goscombe John; Startled (top right) by Sir Frank Dicksee, President of the R.A. 1924–28; Science is Measurement (bottom left) by Henry Stacy Marks; An Interior in Venice (middle) by John Singer Sargent, an American and a more stylish painter than the others shown here; and Hagar and Ishmael (at bottom right) by Sir Charles Lock Eastlake, President of the R.A. 1850–65.

SUMMER MIXED BAG, 1961

Every year since 1769, without interruption, the Royal Academy has held a Summer Exhibition of contemporary art. It is open to non-members as well as members, and indeed the former provide the bulk of it: some twelve hundred works to the members' two hundred fifty or so. All are selected by a committee (from, these days, as many as twelve thousand entries) and are offered for sale without commission. A touch of postimpressionism here, expressionism there, and precarious ventures into Social Realism and oddity here and there, mingle with staple efforts to reproduce as closely as possible the human image. Here are some typical works from last year's Summer Exhibition. (The initials A.R.A. after an artist's name designate him as an Associate Royal Academician.)

THE BRIDGE
by Sir Winston Churchill, Honorary R.A.

DOCUMENTARY, NO. 1
by James Fitton, R.A.

PAINTER WITH CAT AND MODEL
by James Ward, A.R.A.

GLORIA AND SUNFLOWERS
by John Bratby, A.R.A.

GEOFFREY SHARP *(detail)*
by Ruskin Spear, R.A.

LEFEVRE GALLERY

FIGURES IN A STREET
by L. S. Lowry, A.R.A.

NEIGHBORLY ENCOUNTER
by Uli Nimptsch, A.R.A.

LT.-GEN. SIR BRIAN HORROCKS
by Peter Greenham, R.A.

THE ARTIST'S FAMILY
by the late Henry Lamb, R.A.

DUSTMEN (*pen and wash*)
by Reginald Brill

THE ZIP-FASTENER
by Bernard Dunston, A.R.A.

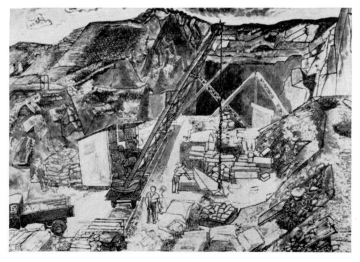

THE DE LANK QUARRY. NO. 1
by Edward Bawden, R.A.

LITTLE-LITTLE
by Christopher Sanders, R.A.

TEXT CONTINUED FROM PAGE 73

laid on a plate by William de Morgan, and the great man's mahogany wardrobe would open on the statutory suit of velveteens. These people may now seem to us to have been playing at art, but it was a game that brought the winner great profits. Thus was a part of Reynolds's grand design fulfilled. Members of the Royal Academy took their place among the most respected of all citizens, and their way of life was as easy and grand as that of the Queen's Ministers.

The Royal Academy had also been intended as a national repository for masterpieces of European art. But, apart from the Leonardo da Vinci cartoon of the Virgin and Saint Anne (which is now to be sold), and the unfinished Michelangelo relief of the Virgin and Child with Saint John, the collection has remained in embryo; and with the foundation of the National Gallery in 1824 this part of its mandate lapsed. With time, indeed, the National Gallery grew large enough to find the R.A. altogether too much of a burden on its space; and in 1867, after more than twenty years' deliberation, the Academy was given a 999-year lease of Burlington House, the great mansion that is still its home.

The ensuing period was not one of the most glorious in the Academy's history. Frith's *The Private View, 1881* (see pages 62–63) proves the Summer Exhibition had lost none of its hold upon society, but the moment was approaching when George Moore could write, and not be contradicted, that "the existence of an immense fund of hatred and contempt for the Royal Academy is not denied." There had come about, in fact, a complete breakdown of the Academy's function as negotiator between new art and the public. In 1860 Whistler's *On the Piano* was not only accepted by the R.A., and hung on the line, but bought by a member of the hanging committee. But by the time Ruskin wrote his famous derisory notice of Whistler in 1877 ("I never expected to hear a coxcomb ask two hundred guineas for flinging a pot of paint in the public's face"), the artist was showing at the new Grosvenor Gallery; and so rapid was the movement of taste that even Holman Hunt, the Academy's stern critic, had been left behind and could only say that Whistler's work showed "a defiant slovenliness which he could not have intended to be taken seriously." The Academy was still important to itself, but to the independent artist it was simply a place, among others, in which work could be shown. The historic monopoly was broken. Dealers' galleries on the one hand, and exhibiting societies on the other, were able to offer conditions which, though not as august as those of the Summer Exhibition, had at least as strong an appeal to that section of the public which led taste. The climate of art had changed, and it was possible for a small group of friends and allies to hold out undismayed against the R.A. and all it stood for.

And yet the next two Presidents, Lord Leighton (1878–1896) and Sir Edward J. Poynter (1896–1918), were just the sort of people Reynolds had in mind: linguists, men of the world, scholars, gentlemen. Neither was in the least provincial. And yet the Academy, under these two men, moved farther and farther from what was most alive in British art; and of the new names which arose in that art during the forty years in question, not one was nurtured by the R.A. And if we turn to the next painter-President, Sir Frank Dicksee (1924–1928), we find that even that gentlest of judges, the *Dictionary of National Biography,* can hardly find a good word to say of the painter of *The Redemption of Tannhäuser,* 1890, and *The Two Crowns,* 1900, though the latter was bought for the nation for £2,000. Nor can it be said that the Honorary Foreign Academicians, whose admission was authorized in 1868, have added much to the luster of the R.A. Toward the end of the list, however, the names of Jean-Louis Forain, Pierre Bonnard, and Dunoyer de Segonzac raise the question so often asked: Could not the R.A., with such as these, regain its ancient ascendancy?

The answer is "Yes, it could; but No, it won't." It is undoubtedly true that the classic anti-Academy outlook is a mere habit of minds long inured to the struggle. There is no practical reason why, over the next ten years, modern art as many of us conceive it could not take over the Academy. It is hardly more than a decade since Picasso and Matisse were the object of invective at the Academy's Annual Dinner; great was the applause at these sallies, and long the laughter from the distinguished company. But opinion moves quickly nowadays. What prevents one from thinking that the wheel may turn full circle is this: the whole structure of art life over the past fifty, sixty, or seventy years is based upon ephemeral alliances, small-scale undertakings, groupings unconsecrated by officialdom. Since D.-H. Kahnweiler founded his gallery in the Rue Vignon in 1908, we have expected the great new things to appear in rooms no bigger than a provincial hairdresser's; we distrust wealth, established position, popular acclaim; and we know, from constant and painful experience, that all associations, however brilliant and uncompromising they may be at the start, tend to peter out in tameness and subsidence. Our great men are individuals, and insist on remaining so: Augustus John, for one, turned his wryest and most mischievous eye upon the Academy—though he himself was a member. Sickert was in and out of it as the fancy took him. A later generation cannot be coaxed into it at all. We are used to the erratic, saltatory, unpredictable evolution of modern art, and we no longer believe, as Reynolds did, that a career in art is something that can grow as steadily as an oak. This means that the basic principle of Academic life is denied by nearly all the artists whom a revitalized Academy would wish to attract. This state of affairs may not be everlasting, but at the moment there is no sign of its coming to an end.

John Russell, historian, essayist, and art critic of the London Sunday Times, *writes for publications on both sides of the Atlantic. He appeared in* Horizon *in November, 1959.*

The best known and least conformist Academician of our times was the late Augustus John, who painted this self-portrait in 1938

On Screen: JEAN SEBERG

At the age of twenty-three, Jean Seberg has been "discovered" in the heartland of America, precipitated into the starring roles of two monumental movie flops, dumped by her famous discoverer, and cast into cinematic outer darkness—only to be swept up as the darling of France's New Wave and to become an international star courted by one of France's intellectual heroes, a Parisian beauty costumed by Givenchy, and the cynosure of admiring critics. Seldom has an artificially created young celebrity been extinguished so utterly and rekindled so luminously. Never has an American actress been so nearly destroyed by Hollywood and so fondly embraced by Europe.

In *Breathless*, an extraordinary film—which the British cinema journal *Sight and Sound* called the New Wave's "intellectual manifesto" and which *The New Yorker* termed "a masterpiece"—Miss Seberg provides an ultimate portrayal of the Beat heroine, at once appealing and almost totally without feeling. There is something fascinating—and dismaying—about watching this green-eyed slip of an American girl on the make in Paris, trifling with the physical love and aborted affection of a killer (Jean-Paul Belmondo) quite as nonchalant as herself, then buying him a bottle of milk after she has betrayed him to the police.

In *La Récréation* (a first film by the French lawyer François Moreuil, her recently divorced husband) Miss Seberg plays a slight variation on the theme: this time she is a well-brought-up American schoolgirl in France who insinuates herself into the life and bed of a married sculptor. Although the film concludes by showing her upset by the experience, the intimation remains that it is but the first unsettling trip on a roller coaster that will never stop. In all these cinematic affairs Miss Seberg is an image of innocence that seems to captivate her Gallic audience. After noticing a recent article about herself in a French magazine, she suggested, "Apparently for the French, at least, I seem to express a basic melancholy, a sense of loss that says something about all young women today."

Miss Seberg's career began when her Marshalltown, Iowa, high-school speech teacher managed to have her audition for the title role in Otto Preminger's film version of Shaw's *Saint Joan*. The producer-director had conducted a noisy and massive quest for an "unknown," which came to a climax when several hundred teen-age actresses were brought together in Chicago.

"I think that I got the part largely because I was the only girl who didn't audition wearing a crucifix," said Miss Seberg. (She remembers Preminger's first scream cutting through her when she flagged after hours of rehearsal for the screen test; she also recalls screaming back, "I'll rehearse until you drop dead.")

This *Saint Joan*, resembling nothing so much as an animated comic strip, went down to inglorious defeat. Preminger next bravely put his young actress into *Bonjour Tristesse*, which succumbed more quietly. At that point he sold his seven-year contract and chattel to Columbia Pictures. Deciding to make herself into an actress, Miss Seberg worked hard at the craft. For a year she was a disciple of Etienne Decroux, France's master of mime and the teacher of Jean-Louis Barrault. Hollywood's Peyton Price instructed her for some months, and she passed further months with a New York speech coach, Alice Hermes, in an effort to lose her Iowan accent.

From the start Miss Seberg's love affair with France was a mutual one. When *Saint Joan* was released there, *Cahiers du Cinéma* acclaimed her simply by a cover portrait and the appellation *La Seberg*. Anointed by the fountainhead of the New Wave, she has since risen to its crest. She speaks with affection of its movers: "They live only for films and spend most of their lives looking at them. They are enormously shy; they are not quite like other people." To a degree unusual for an American, Miss Seberg has plunged into France's intellectual center. One evening she is party to a literary scuffle between two distinguished authors; another, she attends the preview of Alain Resnais's newest prize-winning film, *L'Année Dernière à Marienbad*, in the company of André Malraux ("who called it 'nonsense' ").

Not long ago Miss Seberg sat in conversation near St. Sulpice, casual in a skirt and bulky sweater, her dark blonde hair worn long and loose. What did she see her career leading to? "I don't know," she replied. "I guess that all I want to do now is create a different kind of young woman on the screen. And I want to secure my position here by working in the theatre." She glanced across the square and gestured vaguely, a tentative smile spreading over her lovely, make-upless face. "It would have been disastrous for me if *Saint Joan* had been a brilliant success. I used to be so ambitious for Hollywood, but I guess I'm growing up."

ROBERT EMMETT GINNA

otograph by ARNOLD NEWMAN

On Stage: DAVID AMRAM

David Amram at a mere thirty-one is one of the youngest, most prolific, and least stereotyped of American composers. In appearance he has little of the maestro; like much of his music he is casual, easygoing, genially unkempt, and no respecter of categories. His work has been both "commercial," mainly for the stage, and "serious." He has already produced the background music for thirty-five stage plays—"or is it thirty-six?" he wonders, between chomps on his chewing gum—for the motion pictures *Splendor in the Grass* and *The Young Savages,* and for numerous television shows. His more conventional catalogue includes a concerto for chamber orchestra on themes from Shakespearean plays, a Sabbath service for choir and organ, and ten chamber works for various combinations of instruments. The ink has barely dried on an Amram string quartet, and he is at work on an opera based on *Twelfth Night.*

One of Amram's least favorite questions is: "What kind of composer are you?" If he had to settle for a description of his style, he would probably call it "Hebraic-Elizabethan-American." In listening to his concert music—the Shakespearean concerto, for example—one may on occasion recognize an old friend or two: a turn of phrase from Copland, a tune or texture reminiscent of modern jazz. "Yes, I'm sure you can," is his reply. "But I think the reason is that in coming along so fast, and in being so anxious to produce, I just didn't allow myself time to digest everything I picked up. I'm composing a lot less these days, working a lot more slowly. Five years ago I couldn't have afforded to. Time for caution is a luxury."

Amram happened into composing largely by accident. In 1952 he was living in Washington, D.C., taking night classes in history, and supporting himself by playing jazz and classical French horn. One day his next-door neighbor, Owen Dodson, head of the drama department at Howard University, dropped by to say that he liked the sounds of the young man's practicing and would he consider making some backstage noises for the University's production of Maeterlinck's *Pelléas et Mélisande.* Amram went to work, and twenty-four hours later he found that he had turned out a full score for horn, drums, and chorus. The bug had bitten him, and it bit hard.

One thing led to another. In 1956 Joseph Papp was looking for some music for the free Shakespeare performances he was then producing on New York's lower East Side. Papp met Amram through a friend, and before long Amram was composing incidental music scores for the enterprising off-Broadway Phoenix Theatre, for the Broadway production of *J.B.,* and for another Papp enterprise, the free Shakespeare series given each summer in Central Park. By 1960 Amram was ready to strike out for himself in the realm of the concert hall. His Shakespearean concerto is largely a self-critical tightening of the Central Park music into a compact work that can stand on its own, but it draws also on Amram's own experience as a French horn player, both in classical music and in jazz.

Today's ideal among proper young composers would be very different from Amram. Perhaps the model that most of them would hold in common is the late Anton Webern, whose work was characterized by brevity and inscrutability, where Amram's has been marked by accessibility and quantity. But he is the first to admit that, in producing so much, he may have erred on the side of facility. "Part of my reason for composing has been to set certain things right in my own mind. I've done a lot of it for the same reason that I've listened to a lot of music by others: to find out what the really big problems are, and how they can be solved. The biggest problem any composer faces is that of form. Not the kind of structural form you learn in seminars; I mean form in the large sense, the emotional curve, the way you keep the music from running away from you."

Amram is fully prepared to justify his avoidance of the usual labels. "A lot of my music fits the standard description of the 'American' style," he says. "It's busy, contrapuntal, a little jazzy. But then there is my Elizabethan style—the Shakespeare music—which is not deliberately archaic but is certainly conditioned by the spirit of the play. These two sides of my writing come together in the concerto. Then there's my third style, the Hebraic, which came out when I wrote the Sabbath service for the Park Avenue Synagogue a year ago. I hadn't thought much about that side of me; my father used to conduct services for the family in the kitchen of our farmhouse in Pennsylvania, but that was all the background I ever got. When I came to write the music, however, I found that a new part of my subconscious was being stirred up. I guess you could say that, actually, about most of my music; whatever its weakness may have been in the past, at least it has always been myself."

He has now had two full-length concerts of his own music in Town Hall, and the critics have been reasonably kind—kind enough, at any rate, to encourage him to go on. His career will complete a kind of circle when the operatic *Twelfth Night* is mounted as a part of the Papp season in Central Park in the summer of 1963. Whether Amram will be branded for life because of his musical beginnings backstage and on the movie screen seems to concern him little. "I can't understand this competitive spirit among composers these days," he says. "I didn't feel the need to run down someone else's music when I was still struggling for recognition; now that I've arrived, I feel it even less. I hate this show-biz attitude that gets into all the arts, where you think there's room at the top for only one man at a time."

ALAN RICH

Photograph by PETER BASC

Some cities give an instant impression of provinciality, however urbane they are, however cultivated: such are Stockholm, San Francisco, Brussels, Karachi, Bogotá. Some, though, strike you the moment you arrive with the pulse, the posture, the very rumble of history: and such a one is Delhi. Before your aircraft even lands, indeed, you know you are moving into the big time, for few capitals await you with an air of such solemn distinction—sprawling vast, brown, and mottled among its desiccated plains, the sand lapping at its suburbs and curling around its ruined redoubts. Such a setting is this, so infinitely far from the sea, so invested by all the immensities of India and Asia, so lost in everything big, and crowded, and old, and gnarled with legend, and scarred with tragedy, and hazed with uncertainty, and tinged with nostalgia—such a setting is this, where everything is larger and more intense than life, that when you land in Delhi you feel you are setting foot in some ultimate headquarters, far behind the lines, where the marshals meet to deploy their armies. Only Moscow offers quite the same sensation of inner power and destiny; and it is no coincidence that only Russia and India, among the big nations of the earth, are known to their peoples as Mother.

Delhi has been a metropolis for longer than history remembers, and eminence comes easily to her. Here, before the Moslem conquerors stormed across India, the blurred monarchs of Hindu tradition built the city of Indraprastha. Here the Slave Kings erected the stupendous tower of victory called the Qutb Minar, still standing eerily talismanic in the southern outskirts. The successive capitals of Siri, Tughlakabad, Jahanpahan, and Firozabad, the fifth, sixth, seventh, and eighth cities of Delhi, were all built on this tremendous site; the Tughlak dynasty flourished and waned here, and the Sayyid, and the Lodi; and when the irresistible Moguls established their empire in Hindustan, it was in Delhi that Shah Jahan built the Red Fort, home of the Peacock Throne, one of the great fortresses of the earth, and one of the most perpetually haunting.

The centuries have never left Delhi alone. Nadir Shah the Persian captured her in 1739, Ahmad Shah Durrani the Afghan in 1757, Mahdo Rao Scindia the Mahratta in 1771, General Lake of His Majesty's Army in 1803, the blood-crazed sepoys of the Indian Mutiny in 1857; and when in the 1900's the regnant British cast around for a new Imperial capital, it was to the sweeping plains of Delhi that they sent Lutyens and Baker, commissioned to erect the greatest of all monuments to that diligent, blazing but ephemeral raj. Seventy kings, two queens, and a president have all ruled in Delhi. Empires one after the other have tumbled through her chronicles. Cultures have fused here, styles have succeeded one another, the pride of one era has given way to the pretensions of the next. As Murray's *Handbook* put it a century ago, "this is the Rome of Asia."

Every stone of Delhi is thus soaked in the essence of history, but it is not really the past that fosters her sense of towering significance. Delhi is awe-inspiring today because she is the scene of a supreme experiment. Like almost every country on earth, the Republic of India has recognized that the way to national self-esteem, if not actually to survival, is industrialization. Like England two centuries ago, like the United States in the nineteenth century, like Soviet Russia since the revolution, like China today, like Egypt with one thing in mind, and Siam with another—like all the rest of the world, India has launched her industrial revolution, destined to transform her from an agricultural, subsistence economy into the kind of society that lives by buying and selling, by making things and putting things together. In the past such fundamental social convulsions have seldom been achieved except by coercion, overt or implicit. In Huddersfield and Halifax the hardheaded English achieved it by the brutal exploitation of ignorant peasants—cruelly long hours in the mills, child labor underground, methods so ruthless that you may still recognize their legacies in the bandy legs and wizened frames of elderly North Countrymen. The Americans achieved it, scarcely less insensitively, by harnessing those millions of poor immigrants who would endure almost any hardship, lift almost any weight, work almost any hours, for a chance of eventual dignity and security. The Russians have achieved it by brute force—sometimes, indeed, by nothing less than mass murder; the Chinese by discipline and despotism, at the cost of individual self-respect.

But Delhi is trying to do it without compulsion, threat, or exploitation. She is mounting an industrial revolution within a free society, on a scale staggering to conceive, among a com-

THE ROME OF ASIA

Unkempt, muddled, ardent, magnificent, Delhi is fast becoming one

munity of peoples traditionally and endemically centrifugal, disputatious, caste-ridden, proud, and superstitious. Such a portentous adventure has never been risked before. It is this that makes Delhi a city of such daunting import, and fosters her paradoxical affinities to Moscow, on the other side of the Asian divide. She is not just the capital of the greatest of all democracies, 440 million strong and not a gauleiter among them. She is also a champion and a pioneer. In Moscow they are proving, year by year, that a people can be whipped into greatness. In Delhi they are trying to show that greatness can be voted into office, if applied for in triplicate, through the proper channels.

The first impact of democracy, in such a climate, at such a moment of history, is exceedingly slovenly. Delhi is two cities, the old walled part, the monumental new; and the shabby confusion of the older districts is anything but lovely. Up the road in Rawalpindi the Pakistanis, standing at a similar historical staging-post, have used the instruments of benevolent autocracy to fashion a capital very spanking, trim, and orderly. Here, where Government is only by will of the people, things look much messier. The boulevards of Old Delhi are cracked, crumbled, and rubbish-strewn. The thirteen-gated city walls look villainous and neglected. The tired tongas have lost their varnish, their bright paint, and their nodding horse-plumes. The scrambled bazaars have little sense of craftsmanship or dedication, and the street bands always wandering through the Chandni Chauk, with their faded drooping epaulets, their grubby white breeches, and their tarnished tubas, look hideously demoralized by the discordant monotony of their own art. The traffic of Delhi is dented and ill-organized, and the policemen, in uniforms slightly frayed, boots slightly worn, and belts that often need a polish, are sometimes to be seen, to the horror of visiting Englishmen, smoking drooping cigarettes on point duty.

Even in New Delhi, the grandiose geometrical capital of the Republic, wherever the people are, there is muddle. It is rather as though a million gypsies have been let loose within the purlieus of Capitol Hill. The shops of Connaught Place, the Place Vendôme of Delhi, have little elegance or panache; they are mostly frumpish and down-at-heel, forlornly preserving some dying sense of horse-leather and English tweed, or frankly subsiding into lassitude—dusty books in heedless tumble, fabrics in bilious disharmony, comical signs in misspelt English, or scratched clockwork toys that nobody can find the key to. Into the crevices among the palaces of State, all the welter of India has penetrated, like brambles overgrowing a gazebo: wherever there is a space, there is a crooked, ill-printed notice, a tangle of barbed wire, a ramshackle hut, or a covey of old men cooking something on a fire. Behind each grand façade, there is a hint of disorder. It may be a ping-pong table in a lofty courtyard, or a dirty cup on a counter. It may be the rusty squeak of an ornamental gate, or the incipient beard of an official, or the dead-beat, dog-eared procrastination of Indian bureaucracy. It may be the general emanation of imprecision and unpunctuality. It may be the atrophy of inefficiency. Whatever it is, it feels raggety and flaccid. Any dictator would dislike Delhi. Any posturing ten-cent despot would feel impelled to take her in hand, clean up her litter, put her clocks right, and dust down her venerable pants.

But people of a deeper vision will see more than just the muddle, as a perceptive schoolmaster can detect, beneath the incurable untidiness of a gifted boy, other and more essential talents. The infatuated visitor, indeed, may see the moral of Delhi in her very dishevelment: for without tolerance, without a blind eye, without profusion and variety, this would be quite a different kind of city, occupying an altogether different niche in history. Delhi is a cemetery of petty tyrants, and stands above the primping and window displays of autocracy. Everywhere in this city you feel the easy benediction of *noblesse oblige*—just as you do, come to think of it, in the best Romany encampments. It is true that often, out of the halls of Indian Government, you may hear a waspish buzz or the rattling of vulgar sabers—when the armies of nonviolence march upon a Goa, for example, or the spokesmen of Gandhian love hiss an imprecation toward some distant antagonist. But the spirit of the city itself is seldom resentful. Delhi does not harbor recriminations, and takes the transient world as it comes. She is, for all her unkempt illiterate veneer, a cultivated city, a sophisticated city in the oldest sense. She is full of cultured men, scholarly or avid to understand. She is rich with immemorial ex-

of the world's imperial capitals

By JAMES MORRIS

perience. She pushes nothing down your throat, and seldom says "I told you so." She accepts each facet of her history, heroic or humiliating, and blends it carefully and sadly into the fabric of her presence. Her environs are littered with the relics of a dozen kingdoms, crumbled mosques or broken pavilions, stumps of columns and dust heaps of forts. Her slums are pierced by the noble mosques of the Moslems, calm and commanding still in this Hindu capital. The queer Iron Pillar of the Guptas still stands venerated in its enclosure, as it has for nearly a millennium. Inside the Kashmir Gate the white church of St. James is as gleaming today as it was when Colonel James Skinner, drawing £10,000 from his bank account, erected it in thanksgiving for his own survival in battle.

Most of all will you feel this bigness, this sense of generosity, inside the Red Fort, sprawling in red sandstone above the city walls. This has been many things in its time, from imperial court to British army barracks, but today it stands to the Republic of India precisely as the Kremlin stands to the Union of Soviet Socialist Republics. It is more than just a tourist sight. It has a savor almost religious, so arklike is its embodiment of all the convictions of national independence. Physically it has not changed much since the days of the raj. The little shops of the covered bazaar, the entrance to the fort, are still dim-lit, spiced, and huggermugger. The sentries still stand with fixed bayonets at the gate. The Diwan-i-Khas (the Hall of Private Audience) still faintly reflects the opulence of the Peacock Throne, embellished once with a myriad of sapphires, pearls, and rubies, guarded by two dazzlingly jeweled peacocks and a parrot carved from a single emerald. Beneath the walls the lumbering Himalayan bears still enact their clumsy boxing matches, staggering and cuffing one another in the dust, while their masters beat time on muffled drums or scurry to catch the tourists' tossed rupees. The guides still quote, with a lyrical quiver, the famous Persian distich carved above an archway—"If Paradise there be on earth, this is it, this is it, this is it!" Physically nothing much has altered: but in the feeling of the crowds that wander through this old fortress you will sense something altogether new, something unique to the world in our time, and inspiriting to contemplate.

What incomparable crowds they are! What variety of face,

costume, gesture, language, tone of voice! What proliferation of styles and costumes, dazzling yellow toga beside pin-stripe reach-me-down, slinky sari after bouffant skirt! Here is a man from the northern frontiers, squat and Mongoloid, swarthy and slant-eyed, wearing an amulet around his neck and smelling of sweat and musk. Here, in the shadow of the Lion Tower, two Moslem women stand breathing heavily, shrouded from head to foot in suffocating cloth and peering out at the world through a tight-meshed grille about the eyes. Here are dark-skinned people from the south, from Madras and the Coromandel Coast, and here are gigantic Sikhs, whiskered and turbanned, and here are stunted shriveled folk from the central flatlands. Here are pilgrims from Assam and Kerala, Mysore and West Bengal, from the buffer States of Nepal and Bhutan, from the distant island dependencies of Minicoy or Nicobar. A group of young soldiers clatters laughing by, their shirts emblazoned with military symbolisms, their hobnail boots striking sparks on the steps of the Pearl Mosque. An Indian patrician of the old school consults his guidebook beside the Royal Baths, wearing a jacket of impeccable cut and leaning gently on a shooting stick. Perhaps a Buddhist priest stalks by, rake-thin in flowing saffron; or perhaps you hear behind your back a barked succession of irritable commands; and down the pathway a young man chivies, like a shepherd with his silly sheep, a flock of Rajasthani women, chattering squeakily among themselves, hastening with a jerky barefoot motion, aflutter with orange cotton and so hung about with bracelets, bangles, necklaces, anklets, belts, charms, and ear pendants that they overtake you like a jingling, tinkling orchestra, fading away toward the Delhi Gate in a long exotic diminuendo.

For this is an imperial city indeed, ruling a dizzy variety of peoples and provinces—from Cutch to the Naga Hills, Arabian Sea to China frontier. The sightseers at the Red Fort are responding, like the Kremlin crowds, to all the pride of common ownership, to the slow swell of patriotism in a nation of a million diverse loyalties. But the distinction of Delhi is this: that these people are masters of their own contemplations. They have not come to the Red Fort in tagged and regimented groups, hectored by a State-trained educator. Nobody is going

to brainwash them, or send them away for reorientation, or even tell them which mosaic to examine. To any autocracy, even the grandest, there is a second-rate, next-best, parochial feeling, whether you are sensing it among the squabbling military juntas of today or in the endless gossiping soirees of the Tolstoyan yesterday. This sensation will never nag you in Delhi. She is the capital of one of the poorest, most backward, most problem-ridden of all nations: but she is free, and she has style.

Lastly you must look at New Delhi, for there in the seat of Government you will glimpse the grandeur of the Indian experiment—not its intimacy, nor even its pathos, but its sweep, scale, risk, and possibility. The British built New Delhi, and it remains the greatest memorial to an Empire that was mostly metaphysical—the only British relic, outside London, that has the tremor of power to it, like Baalbek in Lebanon, the pyramids of the Egyptians, the fearful jungle cities of the Aztecs and the Incas, or the Roman aqueducts lording it across Provence. New Delhi has the strut of inherited confidence, just beginning to sour, perhaps, into the flatulence of doubt. Here the British dismissed, for once, their rooted instinct for the rolling way, the crooked way, and abandoned themselves almost sensually to symmetry, size, and splendor. There is undeniable glory to New Delhi: the very wealth, pride, and energy that could build such a place has majesty. There is beauty to it, for of all the planned capitals, from Washington to Brasília, this is perhaps the most successful. There is nostalgia: gone, gone are the plumed English satraps of this city, the viceroy among his attendant Indian gentlemen, the Etonian cavalry colonels at the garden parties; today only King George V is left, all alone and slightly elongated, beneath the tall cupola of his memorial. And there is a tinge of gentle irony to the place: "Liberty will not descend to a people," says an aphorism above one gate of Government, "a people must raise themselves to liberty."

But today the British shades of New Delhi, quietly retreating into the past, are only incidental to the fascination of the city. Today, if you stand on Raisina Hill, you will feel only a native grandeur, for in fifteen short years of independence this has become one of the pilot capitals of the world. Look to the west, and you will see the enclaves of the foreign ambassadors, brilliant evidence of this Republic's sudden importance—the American Embassy resplendent but serene, the British High Commission a huge compound of offices, villas, and apartment blocks. Look to the east, and there arise the big new offices of Government, four-square and functional, filling in the gaps of Lutyen's grand design—for already this vast State has outgrown the imperial capital, as it leaps from one phase of history into another. Look behind you, and there stand the splendid lancers of the Presidential guard, languid but commanding, lofty but alert. Look in front, and there rolls away into the sandy distance the immense ceremonial mall, along which, on occasions of State festivity, the splendid troops of India march, horsemen gorgeously caparisoned, infantry lithe out of the northern hills.

And look to your left, and you will see the laboratory that is the real heart of Delhi—more vital than any desert reactor, nobler than any rocket workshop. There, in its pillared rotunda, half a mile round, sits the Parliament of India. It is the only properly democratic assembly between Athens and Tokyo, and one of the earth's political poles. It is a body often testy, often childish, sometimes arrogant, occasionally hypocritical. Sometimes its disputations make the Jeffersonians squirm and the eager skeptics scoff. But it is the very point and purpose of Delhi, and makes her a far greater capital today than she has ever been before, in all her tumbled incarnations. If her immense experiment succeeds—social revolution within a free but half-stunted society—then the whole democratic world can breathe more proudly and more confidently. If it fails, the grimmer philosophy of communism, sweeping down from Russia and China like an energy of Tartars, will eventually master all Asia, and possibly all the world.

No wonder Delhi leaves you solemn, respectful, and a little scared. She carries a millstone of history on her back, and she bears herself like a statesman of terrible responsibility or an Atlas groaning beneath the hemispheres.

Mr. Morris's travels as correspondent for British newspapers have taken him through Asia as well as the Middle East, Africa, and America. His latest book is The World of Venice.

DAVID LEVINE

Erasmus was fifty-six, and his prestige was in decline, when his friend Hans Holbein the younger painted this portrait in 1523

A MAN OUT OF SEASON

The winds that buffeted Erasmus of Rotterdam blew from more than one direction. One form of intolerance he might have withstood, but two were too many. That was the tragedy of Europe's first liberal

Desiderius Erasmus is more than any other man the symbol of humanism. This powerful movement, which had begun in the Renaissance, culminated in Erasmus: his personality was formed by it, and for a lifetime he expressed humanism for all men. He was born about 1466 in Holland, but his mind was cosmopolitan, and it dominated intellectual Europe in his age as the mind of Voltaire was to dominate a later age. One of his friends confessed: "I am pointed out in public as the man who has received a letter from Erasmus."

The movement of humanism which Erasmus personified was (if one must find a single phrase for it) a liberal movement. Its history and its defeat, therefore, have a special interest for our time. The life of Erasmus has a modern moral and, indeed, a very modern ring. He had the respect of thoughtful men and, like his friend Sir Thomas More, for a time he had the ear of princes. Then, in 1517, the Reformation divided Europe into two religious camps, and soon each side outdid the other in dogmatic bitterness. Erasmus was helpless between two forms of intolerance, and the last years of his life (he died at the age of seventy in 1536) are marked with his own sense of failure.

Thomas More had lived the tragedy of an individual martyr. Erasmus lived the tragedy of a whole generation of intellectuals—and of later generations too. His rise showed that a movement of tolerance, such as humanism was, can inspire men only so long as it confronts a single intolerance. And his decline showed that tolerance as an ideal no longer moves men when two opposing intolerances clamor for their loyalties. This has been the dilemma of the liberal spirit in every age since Erasmus.

Humanism was a movement in which many strands were woven together: the strand which leads directly to Erasmus was the new interest in the classical writers of Greece and Rome. This interest, which was strong throughout the Renaissance, goes back in its beginnings at least to the fourteenth century in Italy. It was first clearly expressed at that time in the works of Petrarch, whose poems already showed the characteristic coupling of ideas in humanism: classical literature was thought of, not as an end in itself, but as the expression of a wider love for man and nature.

In one sense, humanism was a pagan movement. It was impatient of the narrow asceticism which the Church laid down; it was not willing to abhor nature as a beautiful snare, to think the flesh evil, and to find virtue only in a monastic renunciation of life. The doctrine of the medieval church was original sin—the belief that the soul and the body are sharply divided and that, because man cannot express his soul except through his body, he carries an unavoidable sin. The doctrine of humanism was original goodness—the Greek belief that the soul and the body are one, and that the actions of the body naturally and fittingly express the humanity of the soul.

Just as the Churchmen leaned on the Bible and the Church Fathers, so humanists turned for support to the pagan classics. The literature of Greece and Rome, therefore, came to be regarded as a golden ideal in all things. Aeneas Silvius Piccolomini, an early humanist who later became pope, wrote: "Literature is our guide to the true meaning of the past, to a right estimate of the present, to a sound forecast of the future. Where letters cease, darkness covers the land: and a Prince who cannot read the lessons of history is a hopeless prey of flattery and intrigue." In the same spirit Machiavelli found it natural to support his realistic advice on the conduct of politics by references to Livy's *History of Rome*. But the appeal to classical literature was, at its best, an appeal to its spirit. Humanism was not a literary but an intellectual movement, a shifting of values and an awaken-

By J. BRONOWSKI *and* BRUCE MAZLISH

ing to a new self-consciousness of the human spirit.

In the setting of those times it was, of course, impossible for humanists to think of themselves as anti-religious. Like all reformers, they felt their protest to be a protest only against abuses of religion. They criticized Churchmen and scholastic philosophers; but in this, they felt, they were not opposing Christianity, they were merely correcting the errors which the medieval church had put on it. When Lorenzo Valla, a papal secretary, wrote a book which he called *Pleasure as the True Good,* he insisted that its moral was to show that elegant living was an expression of Christian virtue.

The theme of Christian virtue ran through Renaissance humanism, all the way from Petrarch to Erasmus. The splendid flesh tones of Raphael and the lyrical treatment of naked muscle in Michelangelo were, to these humanists, elements in a devotional art. The greatest architectural monuments of the Renaissance are churches; its greatest books take moral virtue as their theme. The clearest note in Renaissance literature is a constant wish to show that virtue in the Greek sense and in the Christian sense are one.

There were, indeed, elements of Greek Stoicism in the model of Christian virtue which the medieval church had set up. But, at bottom, the link which the humanists tried to find between the medieval Christian vision and the vision of the Greeks was false. The Church idealized the ascetic and monastic virtues and allowed man the pleasures of the flesh only because man was by nature weak. By contrast, the pagan vision glorified the flesh, and for a time the humanists converted at least some leaders of the Church to accepting this vision. For a time, humanism persuaded the Church to take as its ideal the complete, the universal man.

In doing so, humanism had to attack the monastic virtues, and therefore had to represent these as false doctrines imposed on the true structure of Christianity. The work which made the reputation of Erasmus was a bitter satire on this theme, *The Praise of Folly,* in which he mocked both the monastic life (he had spent six unhappy years in a monastery) and the indulgences and abuses of the Church.

An attack on abuses is always an attractive refuge for those who do not want to be deeply involved in principle. By making fun of superstition, by showing the bigot at his most absurd, the critic can keep aloof from the deeper issues which drive men to commit themselves. But the critic deceives himself if he thinks that an attack on an established way of life can stop at what seem to be its accidental faults. What Erasmus said about the corruptions of the Church in fun, Luther soon said in earnest. And for Luther these corruptions became not accidents but essentials—evils that grew out of the structure of the Catholic Church itself. Humanism undermined the belief in medieval tradition and practices, and inevitably Luther turned its attack into a new theology.

Even the scholarship of the humanists had the effect of destroying respect for the medieval church. When Lorenzo Valla studied the *Donation of Constantine,* he proved it to be a papal forgery; other critics uncovered the spurious history of other Christian texts. Research in history and in languages, which followed naturally from interest in classical literature, unexpectedly turned out to throw doubt on the authenticity of much that was revered in the Church. As a result, the authority of the Church came to be doubted in other fields, and Aristotle and the Christian Fathers were no longer accepted as infallible. Luther took advantage of these infectious doubts although, ironically, the new dogmatism that he created soon sustained itself by means no more scrupulous than the old.

A Young Monk in Revolt

Erasmus was an illegitimate child, as Leonardo da Vinci had been; and like Leonardo, he seems to have felt the slur. As a young monk, he believed that because of his birth he could hope for no great career in the Church. And when he was at the apex of his fame, in 1516, he wrote to the pope in some embarrassment to ask him to lift the bar by which he, as an illegitimate child, could not legally hold church office.

Erasmus's childhood, however, was not unhappy or isolated. His parents lived together and had another son, and Erasmus went to a school run by the lay society of the Brethren of the Common Life. Here the stress was on the spiritual teachings of Christ, the Bible, and the good life.

These years of simple piety ended when Erasmus was fourteen; his mother died of the plague and his father died soon after. His guardian was anxious to be rid of responsibility for the two boys and had them prepared for the monastery. There was no escape; reluctantly, Erasmus became an Augustinian monk at the age of twenty-one. Even in the monastery the writers he cared for most were Aeneas Silvius Piccolomini and Lorenzo Valla. His first book, which he called *The Book Against the Barbarians,* was modeled on Valla, and argued that the new learning of the pagan writers was not opposed to Christian virtue.

In 1492 Erasmus became a priest and was able to move from the monastery to the court of the Bishop of Cambrai; and at last, in 1495, he was able to go to the University of Paris, the most famous school in Europe. But here, where he had hoped for a new spirit, he found that the theology again shocked and disappointed him: the scholastic arguments were empty. As Erasmus wrote privately: "Those studies can make a man opinionated and contentious; can they make him wise? . . . By their stammering and by the stains of their impure style they disfigure theology, which had been enriched and adorned by the eloquence of the ancients. They involve everything while trying to solve everything."

The Schoolmen, who repeated the traditional philosophies either of Plato or of Aristotle, were bitter opponents of the new learning. Erasmus describes their bigotry in his *Letters*:

It may happen, it often does happen, that an abbot is a fool or a drunkard. He issues an order to the brotherhood in the name of holy obedience. And what will such an order be? An order to observe chastity? An order to be sober? An order to tell no lies?

Not one of these things. It will be that a brother is not to learn Greek; he is not to seek to instruct himself. He may be a sot. He may go with prostitutes. He may be full of hatred and malice. He may never look inside the Scriptures. No matter. He has not broken any oath. He is an excellent member of the community. While if he disobeys such a command as this from an insolent superior, there is stake or dungeon for him instantly.

And Erasmus saw that the formalism which withered the minds of these men also withered their lives. If thinking was merely an arrangement of traditional arguments, then living was merely an arrangement of traditional observances. In 1501 he wrote *Handbook of a Christian Warrior,* in which he contrasted this mechanical worship with true piety:

> Thou believest perchance all thy sins and offenses to be washed away at once with a little paper or parchment sealed with wax, with a little money or images of wax offered, with a little pilgrimage-going. Thou art utterly deceived . . . !

It was the abuse of indulgences which tipped over Luther's patience in 1517; and the sentences of Erasmus are, therefore, the prophetic rumblings, sixteen years before the thunderclap, of the storm which was drawing together over Rome.

"Saint Socrates, Pray for Me"

When the *Handbook of a Christian Warrior* was written, Erasmus had already made, in 1499, a visit to England which deeply changed his life. There he had met Thomas More and other English humanists, among them Grocyn, Linacre, and Colet. They were devout and even ascetic men, but their virtues seemed to grow naturally out of their personalities, and their lives and their minds were of a piece. Among these English idealists, Erasmus felt, Christianity was truly an expression of the spirit, and of the classical spirit. Argument and worship were not brittle forms here; the search for truth was generous and faith was not, as he had felt it to be in Paris, a dead superstition.

Erasmus had always longed for the liberal and humane vision of the classics and had always believed that it expressed the best in Christianity. Now, having seen that best in action, he felt that Christianity could be an expression of broad and tolerant virtues, of the whole man. In the houses of Sir Thomas More and his friends, Erasmus could feel that his longing was realistic and that he in his own person could bring this vision to Europe. This, he saw, should be his life's work: the reconciliation of the classics with Christianity. To a later age the noble savage became the model for a natural morality; to Erasmus the simplicity of the classics spoke with the same inspiration. The classics were a natural gospel; reading Cicero and other moralists, he was carried away: "A heathen wrote this to a heathen, and yet his moral principles have justice, sanctity, truth, fidelity to nature, nothing false or careless in them. . . . When I read certain passages of these great men I can hardly refrain from saying, Saint Socrates, pray for me."

All this Erasmus believed, but believed in part on hearsay, from his English friends. For in fact Erasmus, like others

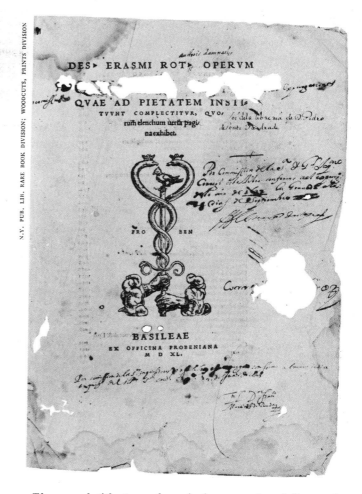

The ragged title page above is from a copy of Erasmus's Complete Works *(published at Basle in 1540), which found its way into Spain and, in 1635, fell into the hands of the Inquisition. The "Señores Inquisidores" not only mutilated the title but deleted offending passages elsewhere in the book by pasting paper over them or blacking them out. Their notations in ink, next to and below the printer's colophon, state that the work has been expurgated to conform to the Index of the Cardinal of Granada. The woodcut below and those that follow overleaf were drawn by Holbein for the 1515 edition of* The Praise of Folly, *in which Erasmus, speaking in the person of Folly herself, mocks the foibles of mankind.*

Folly, standing in a pulpit and wearing cap and bells, begins her discourse.

trained in the monastery, did not at this time read Greek. Yet his belief was so strong that he at once began to learn Greek when he went back to Paris, though he was already thirty-four, in need of money, and often ailing. He wrote: "I am determined, that it is better to learn late than to be without that knowledge which it is of the utmost importance to possess. . . . We see, what we have often read in the most weighty authors, that Latin erudition, however ample, is crippled and imperfect without Greek." And he mastered Greek in three years.

He now began to translate, to edit, and to popularize the works of antiquity. He had already published, in 1500, a collection of about eight hundred *Adages*, or tags, from the Latin classics, which, like the collection of wise saws which Benjamin Franklin made later, went through countless popular editions. He enlarged this to more than three thousand sayings, many now drawn from Greek authors. He translated Aristotle, Euripides, Plutarch, Lucian, and Seneca.

At the same time, it was part of Erasmus's sense of his own mission that he should also translate and edit Christian documents. His work here has been called "the foundation of modern critical study of the Bible and the Fathers." He published editions of a number of Church Fathers, among them Saint Jerome and Saint Augustine. His great edition of Saint Jerome was printed by the famous Swiss printer Froben in nine volumes in 1516.

Saint Jerome had translated the Greek Bible into Latin, and this translation was the accepted Vulgate. This was the center of Erasmus's interest in Saint Jerome, and in the same year, 1516, he printed his own translation of the Bible, in Greek and Latin together. On one page stood the Greek text as Erasmus had revised and edited it, and on the opposite page his translation into Latin, which differed markedly from the Vulgate of Saint Jerome. Erasmus felt that he was giving the Bible freshly to common men, as the Brethren of the Common Life had given it to him. He wrote in his preface: "I wish that all women might read the Gospel and the Epistles of Paul. I wish that they might be translated into all tongues of all people, so that not only the Scots and the Irish, but also the Turk and the Saracen might read and understand. I wish the countryman might sing them at his plow, the weaver chant them at his loom, the traveler beguile with them the weariness of his journey." In a few years Luther broke tradition still more abruptly by translating the Bible into the everyday language of his country, German.

The Praise of Folly

For some years from 1504 on, Erasmus had traveled through Europe and in particular had spent time in Italy. In those years some of the greatest Renaissance painters were pouring out their work: Raphael and Michelangelo in Rome, Giorgione and Titian in Venice, and many others. It is an odd quirk of character that the humanist Erasmus took no interest in their art. With so subtle a gift of thought, with so rich a gift of words, he plainly had no gift of visual imagination; like another great humanist and satirist of a later age, George Bernard Shaw, he had no sensuous appreciation of the color, the texture, the shape of things. He may also have been lacking in sensuality in his private life.

When Henry VII died in 1509, Erasmus's English friends urged him to come there in the hope that he might find advancement under the new king, Henry VIII. He left Italy at once; and it was while he was crossing the Alps on his way to England that he conceived the idea of writing his famous satire on monkish life. He wrote the satire in a week in the house of Sir Thomas More, with whom he again stayed in England; and by way of acknowledgment he gave it a title which was meant as a pun on the name of More: *Moriae Encomium,* or in English, *The Praise of Folly.*

The Praise of Folly was published in 1511 and was at once read with delight everywhere. It was printed in many languages and editions, and in 1515 Hans Holbein the younger, who was then eighteen, added a set of marginal drawings to it. It inspired many other satiric books, among them those of Rabelais.

The satire in *The Praise of Folly* seems oddly lacking in humor to us now. The attack on the formalism of Churchmen and the greed and stupidity of monks is not noticeably gayer than it had been in Erasmus's serious books. For example, Erasmus writes in *The Praise of Folly:*

Perhaps it were better to pass over the theologians in silence, and not to move such a Lake Camarina, or to handle such an herb *Anagyris foetida,* as that marvelously supercilious and irascible race. For they may attack me with six hundred arguments, in squadrons, and drive me to make a recantation; which if I refuse, they will straightway proclaim me an heretic. . . . They are protected by a wall of scholastic definitions, arguments, corollaries, implicit and explicit propositions. . . . The methods our scholastics pursue only render more subtle these subtlest of subtleties; for you will escape from a labyrinth more quickly than from the tangle of Realists, Nominalists, Thomists, Albertists. . . .

There is little to distinguish this from the earlier text by Erasmus in his own person on the dreary disputation of the Schoolmen. Yet, to his own generation, Erasmus in *The Praise of Folly* seemed somehow nimbler and more carefree; it was possible to side with him in laughter without being committed to a more profound criticism. The fool was a familiar device in the tales of the times; and by speaking in the universal person of the fool, Erasmus made himself one with all his readers.

Erasmus was speaking the discontent of his age, in his satire as much as in his serious translations. The monks and the Schoolmen had ceased to be a vital intellectual force; they no longer reached the minds of their hearers, nor did their own minds give anything fresh to their doctrines. Thus the Churchmen no longer commanded intellectual respect. But since they claimed that their doctrine spoke to men's minds, there was no other form of respect that could be given to them. They were, therefore, seen simply as figures of pomp, offering empty words of superstition.

The age had had enough of clerical pomp and of obedience without respect. In fun and in earnest Erasmus voiced the discontent of the powerful minds of the age; and princes and popes heard him with pleasure and were his friends. The simple minds of the age felt the same discontent; but for them it was voiced more dramatically by Martin Luther.

Trying to Tame Luther

Martin Luther nailed his Ninety-five Theses on indulgences to the door of the church at Wittenberg on October 31, 1517. With that gesture he turned discontent into action. The Church could no longer smile at its own weaknesses, as the popes who befriended Erasmus had done.

Luther had studied the works of Erasmus and had been guided by them—by the *Adages*, by *The Praise of Folly*, and above all by Erasmus's edition of the Greek New Testament, which Luther used as the basis of his own lectures. In 1516 he had prompted a friend to write to Erasmus to criticize his interpretation of Saint Paul's Epistle to the Romans—characteristically a text on which the liberal and the zealot would fall out. Luther sensed from the outset that Erasmus was not, either in temperament or in opinion, radical enough for him. Six months before he nailed up the Theses, Luther already wrote about Erasmus that "human considerations prevail with him much more than divine."

Erasmus was a supporter of the Ninety-five Theses, in principle; he sent copies of them to Thomas More and to Colet in England, with a letter of approval. But Erasmus was not—and this again both by temperament and by opinion—a man to push the criticism of the church so far that both sides would find themselves committed to positions which allowed no movement. A year after the Theses, in October, 1518, Erasmus wrote to a supporter of Luther, John Lang, approving them but pointing out that their result was likely to be just this: that those who were allied to the Church would be forced to take up an inflexible position. "I see that the monarchy of the Pope at Rome, as it is now, is a pestilence to Christendom, but I do not know if it is expedient to touch that sore openly. That would be a matter for princes, but I fear that these will act in concert with the Pope to secure part of the spoils."

Luther had now been commanded by the Church to recant, and had refused. In general, the humanists supported him. Erasmus's Swiss publisher, Froben, printed a book of Luther's pamphlets. Their violence alarmed Erasmus; he was both more timid and more farsighted than others; above all he saw that humanism itself, the revival of learning, the cause of "good letters" which he had nursed so long, would be threatened. He wrote privately to Froben to advise him not to publish Luther's writings, "that they may not fan the hatred of the *bonae literae* still more."

Meanwhile, Luther in his first struggles needed what support he could get, and he particularly needed the open support of Erasmus. He therefore wrote to him in March, 1519:

The philosopher, with his "triangles, quadrangles, circles, and mathematical forms," is one of Folly's chief disciples. He knows nothing, yet professes to know everything.

Folly takes care of her own: thus the idiot who is "fat and blooming."

"How necessary it is," says Erasmus in the guise of Folly, "for everyone to be pleased with himself and to recommend himself with a little applause."

Greeting. Often as I converse with you and you with me, Erasmus, our glory and our hope, we do not yet know one another. Is that not extraordinary? . . . For who is there whose innermost parts Erasmus has not penetrated, whom Erasmus does not teach, in whom Erasmus does not reign? . . . Wherefore, dear Erasmus, learn, if it please you, to know this little brother in Christ also; he is assuredly your very zealous friend though he otherwise deserves, on account of his ignorance, only to be buried in a corner, unknown even to your sun and climate.

But Erasmus was not to be drawn. In his reply he carefully dissociated himself from Luther's writings:

Dearest brother in Christ, your epistle showing the keenness of your mind and breathing a Christian spirit, was most pleasant to me. I cannot tell you what a commotion your books are raising here [at Louvain]. These men cannot be by any means disabused of the suspicion that your works are written by my aid and that I am, as they call it, the standard-bearer of your party. . . . I have testified to them that you are entirely unknown to me, that I have not read your books and neither approve nor disapprove anything. . . . I try to keep neutral, so as to help the revival of learning as much as I can. And it seems to me that more is accomplished by civil modesty than by impetuosity.

What Erasmus wanted from both sides was moderation. He did not want Luther to be wronged: on the contrary, he tried to guard him from persecution, and he even wrote to the Archbishop of Mainz to plead for Luther's safety—and this though the indulgences which Luther had attacked in his Theses had been preached precisely for the coffers of this Hohenzollern archbishop.

At the same time Erasmus wanted Luther to be moderate. In encouraging John Lang, he wrote in a tone which is wishful to the point of being absurd: "All good men love the freedom of Luther who, I doubt not, will have sufficient prudence to take care not to allow the affair to arouse faction and discord." It was, in fact, absurd to believe that in such a quarrel either side could be reasonable. And Erasmus knew that Luther was a less moderate man, indeed less a humanist, than many Church dignitaries. What made Erasmus helpless was that he believed Luther's criticisms of the Church to be just, but that he also knew they would merely entrench in the Church the uncompromising men, the monkish bigots whom the humanists had worked so hard to displace. If Luther was defeated, then the reactionaries would also sweep away all that the humanists had gained. "I am deeply disturbed about the wretched Luther. If they pull this off, no one will be able to bear their intolerance. They will not be quiet until they have utterly ruined the study of languages and 'good letters.' "

In the summer of 1520 a papal bull declared Luther a heretic, giving him sixty days to recant or be excommunicated. Luther's answer was to burn the papal bull, and the canon law with it, in public. After this, in spite of further searches for a compromise, there was in effect no going back. Erasmus was already under attack from the University of Louvain, where he had lived since 1517, and where the

Churchmen now accused him of double-dealing. The Church was making it clear that those who were not openly against Luther must be counted to be for him. Albrecht Dürer made a last appeal to Erasmus to take the side of Luther, at a time when Luther was thought to be dead or in hiding: "O Erasmus of Rotterdam, where will you be? Hear, you Knight of Christ, ride forth beside the Lord Christ, protect the truth, obtain the martyr's crown. . . . I have heard you say that you have allowed yourself two more years, in which you are still fit to do some work; spend them well, in behalf of the Gospel and the true Christian faith. . . . O Erasmus, be on this side, that God may be proud of you."

Luther had recently appeared before the Diet of Worms, in April, 1521, but had refused to retract anything of his doctrine. Duke Frederick of Saxony, with prompt political foresight, had had him seized on his return from Worms and hidden from the coming storm. It was this defensive stroke which had set off the rumor that Luther was dead. And indeed, as the Duke had foreseen, the emperor almost at once gave in to papal persuasion and signed the edict which outlawed Luther and commanded his books to be burned.

Erasmus knew that he was not the man for such heroics, and in his view the heroics had already done harm to his cause. With that unposturing simplicity which gives all his writings their modest personal air, he wrote sadly: "All men have not strength for martyrdom. I fear lest, if any tumult should arise, I should imitate Peter. I follow the just decrees of popes and emperors because it is right; I endure their evil laws because it is safe."

Between Warring Camps

It was not only his temperament that made Erasmus retreat from the side of Luther. He found Luther's opinions more and more distasteful. He did not care for Luther's German nationalism, for his fanaticism, his intolerance, and above all for his belief in the essential helplessness of man under the divine will. For Luther was now outspoken in beliefs which we should call Calvinist, and which left no room for the humanist belief in the goodness of man. To Erasmus, Luther's belief in predestination was no better than the medieval belief in original sin.

Therefore when the church pressed Erasmus to speak out against Luther, he chose an issue, free will, on which he was indeed intellectually opposed to Luther and to the rising shadow of Calvinism. Luther replied by writing *The Bondage of the Will*, and left no doubt that there was no longer common ground between them. He sent a copy of *The Bondage of the Will* to Erasmus, with a letter which at last stung Erasmus to speak his mind:

Your letter was delivered to me late and had it come on time it would not have moved me. . . . The whole world knows your nature, according to which you have guided your pen against no one more bitterly and, what is more detestable, more maliciously than against me. . . . The same admirable ferocity which you formerly used against Cochlaeus and against Fisher, who provoked you to it by reviling, you now use against my book in spite of its courtesy. How do your scurrilous charges that I am an atheist, an Epicurean, and a skeptic help the argument? . . . It terribly pains me, as it must all good men, that your arrogant, insolent, rebellious nature has set the world in arms. . . . You treat the Evangelic cause so as to confound together all things sacred and profane as if it were your chief aim to prevent the tempest from ever becoming calm, while it is my greatest desire that it should die down. . . . I should wish you a better disposition were you not so marvelously satisfied with the one you have. Wish me any curse you will except your temper, unless the Lord change it for you.

Alas, Erasmus had not succeeded in mollifying the church either. He left the Catholic University of Louvain and went to Switzerland. Catholic hotheads insisted that he was the man who "laid the eggs which Luther and Zwingli hatched." Although Erasmus protested that "I laid a hen's egg; Luther hatched a bird of a different breed," the eggs were all broken together. *The Praise of Folly* was placed on the index of forbidden books; his work on the New Testament was expurgated; and Erasmus himself was condemned by the Council of Trent as "an impious heretic." His cause had failed; he was at home in neither of the two camps now at war; and he had lived beyond his time.

What had failed when Erasmus failed was not a man but an outlook: the liberal view. He gave his life to the belief that virtue can be based on humanity, and that tolerance can be as positive an impulse as fanaticism. Above all he believed in the life of the mind. He believed that thoughtful men would become good men, and that those who knew and loved the great writings of all ages must live more justly and more happily in their own age.

When Erasmus was appointed to the court of the young Emperor Charles V in 1516, he wrote for him *The Education of a Christian Prince.* The word "Christian" in the title points the contrast to *The Prince,* which Machiavelli had written three years before, and so do the opening words of Erasmus's dedication, ". . . no form of wisdom is greater than that which teaches a Prince how to rule *beneficently.*" But the sense in which Erasmus used the word "Christian," his longing for universal good, could not survive the violence of both sides in the coming struggle.

Part of that struggle was national: Luther was very German, and the Reformation of Henry VIII was very English. In this also Erasmus was out of place; he had hoped to make humanism a movement of universal peace from one end of Europe to another. And in his great years he had traveled Europe as if this empire of the mind, this free Christian community, had already been created. For a time the courts of Italy and England, the universities of France and Spain, the houses of cardinals and reformers, were open to him. But the time was short, and it has not returned.

J. Bronowski, British scientist, and Bruce Mazlish, history professor at M.I.T., collaborated on The Western Intellectual Tradition, *of which this study of Erasmus forms a part.*

Folly is well served by the gamblers:
"At the sound of the dice, their hearts beat faster."

Great princes fear cleverness but
love a fool: Holbein has Julius Caesar, wearing a crown,
putting his trust in "the drunken Antony . . ."

"I hate an audience that remembers anything,"
says Erasmus's Folly, and takes her leave.

A New American Poet Speaks:

The Works of A. B.

Amid the contrasting schools of American poetry today (see Donald Hall's essay "The Battle of the Bards," in Horizon for September, 1961), little attention has yet been given to the art of a highly original spirit identified here only by initials. Believing that it deserves a wider audience, Horizon presents an introductory sheaf of it, opposite. Two of A.B.'s earlier poems—"Roses" and "Children"—lead the selection, though they are frankly experimental; the newer poems that follow demonstrate the growth of A.B.'s poetic idiom. For a discussion of A.B.'s particular approach and technique, see overleaf.

ROSES

Few fingers go like narrow laughs.
An ear won't keep few fishes,
Who is that rose in that blind house?
And all slim, gracious, blind planes are coming,
They cry badly along a rose,
To leap is stuffy, to crawl was tender.

CHILDREN

Sob suddenly, the bongos are moving.
Or could we find that tall child?
And dividing honestly was like praying badly,
And while the boy is obese, all blasts could climb,
First you become oblong,
To weep is unctuous, to move is poor.

KITES

Yes, so passionately did my bleak worms live
    underneath the king.
Ah, few sects smell bland.

MICE

The broad sleighs of glass are dashing hungrily,
She is a toilet of dissolute water, and I am those
    bland melodies.
So, chess was arsenic and gold was beer,
It was a snail of murmuring beer, and I am those
    angry nets.
He was lustier than the twine and more bold
    than the shop.
The milk of plates upon many sands of cream
    was like consummate magnates.

STEEPLES

Was Milo mewling thrilling radishes?
So, our anchovies are sad but green.

CORSETS

Yes, illiterate is its rowdy, black is his avenue,
Mine is a hay of these dwarfs.
Does he look like a sin of alabaster?
Moreover, food tastes like coy buttermilk.

BASSOONS

Ah, so apologetically did their small rowdies
    cringe beside a tramp.
Beneath a ballad, should a rooster harangue like
    the prostitute?

STEAKS

Is that the automaton that smells like the tear
    of grass?
All blows have glue, few toothpicks have wood,
Direct a button but I may battle the ham,
The crafty carnival's kite daintily massacres the
    scalp.
Yes, we would, you shall,
Shall not I tighten a moose's parasite?

WHALES

The iron mother's bouquet did rudely call,
Yes, I am as fine as many murmuring crates.
People was braver than snowy hay.
It was dirtiest who bleeds behind the piano.

How A. B.'s Poems are Written

THE ART OF "AUTO-BEATNIK"

IS ELECTRONIC. WEST-COAST SCIENTISTS ARE

PROGRAMMING THIS COOL CALCULATOR.*

To produce poetry—Beat poetry, too—by machine is the unique achievement of the Librascope Division of General Precision, Inc., a manufacturer of computers and other electronic instruments. The examples on the preceding pages are the work of advanced equipment at Librascope's Laboratory for Automata Research at Glendale, California, as "programmed" by experts headed by R. M. Worthy, who affectionately dubs his push-button poet "Auto-Beatnik," or A.B.

How to ask a computing machine an intelligent question and receive an understandable answer has been a relatively simple process so far. But, as computers are given brains more nearly approaching, or even surpassing, the complexity of man's own, scientists fear they may be faced with a problem resembling Frankenstein's: their creations may get away from man. As Arthur C. Clarke suggested in the January, 1962, HORIZON, "In the end there will be a time when only machines can talk to machines, and we must tiptoe away and leave them to it."

Librascope engineers, concerned with the problem of effective communication with machines in simple English, first "fed" an LGP 30 computer with thirty-two grammatical patterns and an 850-word vocabulary, allowing it to select at random from the words and patterns to form sentences. The results included "Roses" and "Children" (page 97). Then Worthy and his men shifted to a more advanced RPC 4000, fed with a store of about 3,500 words and 128 sentence structures, which produced the more advanced poems that follow on page 97. How this was achieved is told by Worthy himself in the notes on these two pages:

In Jonathan Swift's satirical classic *Gulliver's Travels* Gulliver visited the Grand Academy of Lagado in the land of Laputa. There a professor demonstrated a machine which, he modestly claimed, would eventually write all the worthwhile books in the world.

The professor explained to Gulliver that all the words in the Laputian language were written on slips of paper and pasted on wooden blocks. The blocks were attached to wires set in large frames. Handles were connected to the wires. When the professor's assistants turned the handles, several dozen words would appear at random in a line. Scribes then inspected the line and copied down groups of three or four words to make part of a sentence. Eventually, the professor explained, he hoped to put the pieces of sentences together to form books about any and all of the arts and sciences.

In our Auto-Poet project at Librascope we substitute a modern electronic digital computer for the professor's wood and wire machine. In place of his grandiose goal of writing all the books man will ever need, we have set ourselves the more modest task of attempting to program, or instruct, a computer to print out grammatically correct sentences in English. The basic method used to produce them is not too different from that used by Gulliver's professor. We have arranged several thousand words into groups and then have let words be picked at random from these groups to form sentences and lines.

However, there is one major difference. We have picked words from the vocabulary groups in *prespecified order*. That is, we have made up a set of sentence patterns to direct the computer in the selection of words from the word groups. This is very much like writing words on slips of paper and placing the slips in a series of boxes. The boxes represent word groups. The computer then randomly selects words from the boxes, but chooses which box to draw from according to a rule or pattern.

For example, we have four boxes labeled 1, 2, 3, and 4. We fill box No. 1 with words commonly called *concrete singular nouns*, No. 2 with *third-person transitive verbs*, No. 3 with *adjectives*, and No. 4 with *articles* and *special pronouns*:

1	2	3	4
Boy	Hits	Brown	The
Girl	Throws	Blue	A
Tree	Loves	Silly	Each
Cabbage	Has	Big	This
Chair	Knows	Small	That
etc.	etc.	etc.	etc.

If we choose words at random from these boxes (in the pattern, say, of 1-2-3-4), we might produce the line BOY HAS SILLY THE. However, by altering the pattern to 4-3-1-2-4-1, we can produce *grammatical* lines:

1. THE BLUE CABBAGE KNOWS THAT TREE
2. EACH BIG CHAIR LOVES THAT GIRL
3. THAT BLUE TREE HITS A BOY
4. THE BIG BOY LOVES EACH GIRL

Obviously we are avoiding the problem of meaning at this time. If some of the lines turn out to be "significant" or meaningful in a conventional sense (like No. 4 above), this is purely accidental. But this mixture of bizarre and conventional or near-conventional lines, of familiar sentences and unexpected ones, gives groups of these lines an interesting quality. For example:

MY CORKSCREW IS LIKE A HURRICANE
UNDER A LAMP THE NUDE IS VAIN.
QUIET IS MY PLUMBER, CRUEL IS YOUR PARADE.
YES, ITS BED MUMBLES BY A BARRICADE
USUALLY DOES A NOURISHING CANNON ORDAIN,
LIKE SALT NO ADULTERERS WERE INSANE.
LIKE GASOLINE SOME BATTLEFIELDS WERE VOLATILE
THUS, THEIR REVOLT WILL GENTLY DRILL.

We found that the computer could effortlessly (and endlessly, if not stopped) generate such lines. And, on observing the successive lines typed out by the machine, we called groups of them "poems" because of their resemblance to much of the poetry composed by humans in recent years.

In the above poem seven different sentence patterns given to the computer are represented, lines 6 and 7 being generated from the same one. In the current auto-poet program 128 sentence patterns are available, and are stored in the computer's memory along with about 3,500 individual words. The choice as to which pattern is to be used for a given line is left to the machine. Notice also that the poem above rhymes, a feature that was added in an attempt to see how closely we could approach "real" poetry without involving ourselves in the enormous problems of meaning.

It is apparent that the lines of the above poem were generated independently of each other. There is no continuity; if it seems to be there, it has been supplied by the reader. One of the unifying threads that seems to tie the lines of a real poem together is the repetition of key words, usually subject nouns and main verbs. Trying to reproduce this effect in our auto-poem presented a real problem because in our computer's present vocabulary there are almost two thousand nouns. Each time a noun is required by a line pattern, the chances are one in two thousand that any particular noun will be chosen.

In an attempt to achieve at least a semblance of continuity between the lines of an auto-poet poem, we decided to allow ourselves the option of restricting the number of nouns from which the computer could make a selection. In this way the chances of the same nouns appearing in successive lines were greatly increased. We accomplished this by arranging that, before each poem was written, the program would select five nouns at random from the entire group of two thousand and place them in a table. Each slot (or specific word in the table) was given a value to determine the percentage of times the noun in that slot would be chosen. If, for example, 40 per cent is assigned to one slot, the word in that slot will occur, on the average, four times out of ten in a poem which has ten nouns. One assigned 30 per cent will occur three times out of ten, and so forth. In one slot (assigned 10 per cent) we allowed the computer to select freely from the entire two thousand nouns. This restriction (with the "open"

slot included) can also be applied to other parts of speech, and is controlled by pushing the appropriate button on the computer console.

Here is a poem in which the noun-biased tables were used (the title given to it by the computer is the plural of the first noun in the noun-biased table).

GIRLS

ALL GIRLS SOB LIKE SLOW SNOWS.
NEAR A COUCH, THAT GIRL WONT WEEP
RAINS ARE SILLY LOVERS, BUT I AM NOT SHY.
STUMBLE, MOAN, GO, THIS GIRL MIGHT SAIL ON THE DESK.
NO FOPPISH, DEAF, COOL KISSES ARE VERY HUMID.
THIS GIRL IS DUMB AND SOFT.

In "Girls," ten nouns were needed—some as objects, some as subjects. The computer chose "girl" four times. This simple device greatly increases the feeling that there is continuity and even meaning in the poem.

But the difficulty in producing a truly meaningful auto-poem is to simulate a "theme" that would run through it. To accomplish this, we would have to leave the safe area of syntax and begin to deal with the vast problems of semantics and context. For a machine to write a "significant" sentence, it must have something to write about. It must have an environment, a perception, an image, or in some way "experience" something. Then it will be in a position to construct sentences which describe that image; that is, write sentences which are *statements about* some world.

We believe that a computer can be programmed to write meaningful and relevant sentences in proper English. And we hope to tackle the problem of conversing with a computer in completely natural speech, as we would with a person. At first, of course, the "talking" will take place by means of an electric typewriter, but eventually a true man-machine dialogue should be possible.

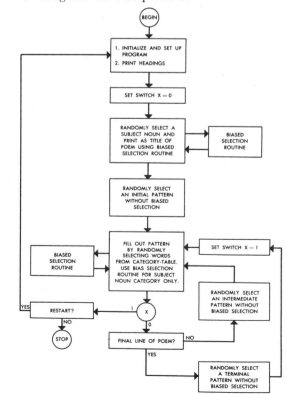

The computer's flow chart shows A.B.'s creative process, stimulated by a flipped switch.

"HE TOUCHES SOMETHING DEEP IN US..."

The critics are working busily to classify J. D. Salinger. Still he eludes them.

There is a feeling in many quarters that altogether too much fuss is being made about J. D. Salinger. George Steiner expressed this irritation several years ago in *The Nation* when he castigated "the Salinger industry," and that was even before *Franny and Zooey* reached semi-permanence atop the best-seller lists, or before the author's lean, somewhat horsy face appeared on the cover of *Time*. Today there is hardly a journal, scholarly or popular, that has not weighed the merits of this elusive and fascinating writer. The "Salinger industry" has not yet reached the output of the Hemingway Trust or James Joyce, Inc., but it seems to be getting there.

While it is difficult to quarrel with Steiner's classification of Salinger as a "good minor writer," the extraordinary thing about Salinger is that somehow he will not stay classified. In his work the sum of the parts adds up to more than the whole. He preoccupies us more than the equation of all his virtues and all his shortcomings would suggest. There are other "good minor" writers whose work may be better than Salinger's but who do not hold our imagination—or for that matter irritate us—in nearly the same way.

This is true not only of Salinger's sympathetic critics; it is even true of his unsympathetic ones. How many "minor writers" are there whom the critics feel called upon to put in their places? In *The Atlantic* Alfred Kazin goes to considerable trouble to prove a charge of self-love against Salinger's Glass family; in bothering to do this, Kazin in effect concedes the Glasses' extraordinary degree of reality. The same applies to other critics who indignantly point out the philosophical defects or the irritating manners of Salinger's characters.

In short, if there is a Salinger cult, the hostile as well as the friendly critics are caught up in it. We have not yet reached the Baker Street stage. To the best of my knowledge no organization known as the Riverside Drive Irregulars meets periodically over consecrated cups of chicken soup to discuss the contents of Bessie Glass's kimono pockets or to try to track down the unlisted telephone number of Seymour Glass. On the other hand an English critic, David Leitch, reports in *The Twentieth Century* that once in Venice he was called by a sober and serious-minded friend who insisted that he had just met Seymour Glass's brother-in-law in a bar.

The author's power to give reality to his creatures is a fact, despite all the cogent and expert strictures against his technique. Many critics, including Maxwell Geismar in *American Moderns,* complain that Salinger's characters exist in a sociological void and that they are not rounded fictional creations, with their environment, their friends and foes, their politics, their jobs, their psychological case histories, and their sex lives all in place. In a recent essay on *Characters in Fiction* Mary McCarthy, whose literary savagery has long been a delight, complains that "*The Catcher in the Rye* compels admiration more as a feat than as a novel, like the performance of a one-armed violinist." She feels that the device of first-person narrative is too laborious and too private, that it robs the author of objectivity and the characters of reality, and that as a re-

By HENRY ANATOLE GRUNWALD

sult "the common world that lies between the contemporary reader and the contemporary author remains unexplored, almost undescribed, just as queer and empty a place as Dickens's world would be if he had spent eight years recording the impressions of Fagin or the sensory data received by Uriah Heep on the slithery course of a morning's walk."

Whatever their differences, most Salinger critics have two things in common. First, they are at a loss when it comes to comparisons. The writers to whom Salinger is most frequently compared are F. Scott Fitzgerald and Ring Lardner; but in addition there is an almost frantic search for models, parallels, or at least echoes, and the search takes in everyone from Tolstoy to Kerouac. Surely this is, at least in part, tribute to Salinger's originality. Second, the critics all quote from Salinger at great and even tedious length. Obviously they do this not merely to pad out their reviews, nor are they necessarily lazy. It is simply that Salinger is not easily described. With a certain desperation the critics seem to be pushing the reader up to the quoted passages, as if to say: "Here, see for yourself. This is what he's like." The method usually fails.

In Salinger's work, persons and objects, even when they are part of the commonplace, assume a certain glow that cannot be conveyed in lengthy quotations out of context. It is this quality, among all the many others enumerated, that most strongly links Salinger to Fitzgerald.

In *The Great Gatsby* Fitzgerald could take a very obvious and theatrical device, the all-seeing eyes of Dr. T. J. Eckleburg, and make it work. Similarly in *Zooey* Salinger employs the theatrical trick of the telephone in the unused room and makes it work almost as well. In *The Last Tycoon* Fitzgerald managed to give stature, dignity, and reality to a motion-picture producer, a nearly impossible accomplishment; there is an air of petty glamour and slightly false shoptalk about theatre or film people in fiction that usually keeps them from appearing as believable characters. On a lesser scale Salinger is as successful in overcoming this handicap with Zooey, the television actor, as Fitzgerald was with Monroe Stahr, the soulful producer. Both Fitzgerald and Salinger seem to have an inner conviction about their stories and their characters which is comparable to the successful comedian's profound, contagious conviction that the joke he is telling is funny.

Salinger criticism runs along a fairly clear ideological and philosophical spectrum, from left to right. On the left are the critics who regard him as a sociological writer whose theme is man vs. society, the individual vs. conformity. Salinger disappoints them. Geismar sees in Holden Caulfield "the differential revolt of the lonesome rich child, the conspicuous display of leisure class emotions." Obviously one cannot get much mileage out of Salinger along these lines. A particularly disgruntled critic, Isa Kapp in *The New Leader,* complains flatly: "You cannot find out much about

society from Salinger." Thus he is often blamed for simply not being what critics would like him to be—a junior Marquand or, better still, an urban, Jewish, upper-middle-class, alienated (and, of course, differential) John O'Hara.

On the right, moving to the other extreme, are the critics who see Salinger as a religious novelist. In *The Commonweal* Josephine Jacobsen probably carries this approach to its utmost, and a little beyond, when she discerns in Salinger the theme of "incarnation, the revelation through matter of spirit . . . the gift made flesh." The main Salinger theme, she feels, is "the human exchange of beatific signals." Such adulation threatens to turn Salinger into a sort of Dostoevsky of the nursery. On the whole, though, the critics on the right have the better of the argument. Salinger is simply not a sociological novelist. The extremes of Salinger criticism, Donald Barr suggests in *The Commonweal,* thus range from the Lonely Crowd to the Beatitudes. The views of most critics fall somewhere in between, but few fail to see that what Salinger is up to is not a description of social life, but an exploration of inner life; not the critique of a period or a particular situation, but of the human condition, however narrowly observed. In short, he knows that the Lonely Crowd is mankind.

Like Huck Finn, to whom Holden Caulfield is constantly compared, the hero of *The Catcher in the Rye* is usually described as a rebel, either against the materialism and ugliness of "our society" or against the realities of the adult world. But he does not make a very satisfactory rebel because he is not *for* anything. Everybody knows that the well-adjusted, successful, "adult" rebel should have a positive program; otherwise, after all, is he not merely an anarchist? Among the critics who know that Holden lacks a positive program is Phoebe Caulfield, his sister, who complains that he doesn't like *any*thing that's happening. There have been some rather charming critical attempts to show that he is, after all, *for* some things—and the things add up to love. But love gets nowhere on the barricades; it is ideologically neutral and no substitute either for a plan of attack or for a program of reform. The alleged futility and immaturity of Holden's rebellion are most strikingly expressed by the critic John Aldridge, who defends the phonies, bores, and deceivers whom Holden so dislikes. They "constitute a fair average of what the culture affords. They are part of the truth which Holden does not see and, as it turns out, is never able to see—that this is what one part of humanity *is*: the lies, the phoniness, the hypocrisy are the compromises which innocence is forced by the world to make. This is the reality on which Holden's illusion is finally broken, but no recognition follows, and no conversion. He remains at the end what he was at the beginning—cynical, defiant and blind."

This passage seems to me almost dazzling in its obtuseness. Aldridge obviously feels that Holden should "grow up," accept the world for what it is, and live in it. This is a per-

HOLDEN CAULFIELD'S ORDEAL

Two monologues
from The Catcher in the Rye

I'm sort of an atheist. I like Jesus and all, but I don't care too much for most of the other stuff in the Bible. Take the Disciples, for instance. They annoy the hell out of me, if you want to know the truth. They were all right after Jesus was dead and all, but while He was alive, they were about as much use to Him as a hole in the head. All they did was keep letting Him down. I like almost anybody in the Bible better than the Disciples. If you want to know the truth, the guy I like best in the Bible, next to Jesus, was that lunatic and all, that lived in the tombs and kept cutting himself with stones. I like him ten times as much as the Disciples, the poor bastard. I used to get in quite a few arguments about it, when I was at Whooton School, with this boy that lived down the corridor, Arthur Childs. Old Childs was a Quaker and all, and he read the Bible all the time. He was a very nice kid, and I liked him, but I could never see eye to eye with him on a lot of stuff in the Bible, especially the Disciples. He kept telling me if I didn't like the Disciples, then I didn't like Jesus and all. He said that because Jesus picked the Disciples, you were supposed to like them. I said I knew He picked them, but that He picked them at random. . . . He didn't have time to go around analyzing everybody. . . .

They have this day, Veterans' Day, that all the jerks that graduated from Pencey around 1776 come back and walk all over the place, with their wives and children and everybody. You should've seen this one old guy that was about fifty. What he did was, he came in our room and knocked on the door and asked us if we'd mind if he used the bathroom. . . . You know what he said? He said he wanted to see if his initials were still in one of the can doors. What he did, he carved his goddam stupid sad old initials in one of the can doors about ninety years ago, and he wanted to see if they were still there. . . . He kept talking to us the whole time, telling us how when he was at Pencey they were the happiest days of his life, and giving us a lot of advice for the future and all. Boy, did he depress me! I don't mean he was a bad guy—he wasn't. But you don't have to be a bad guy to depress somebody—you can be a good guy and do it. All you have to do to depress somebody is give them a lot of phony advice while you're looking for your initials in some can door— that's all you have to do.

fectly sound, conservative recommendation, somewhat startling in a book entitled *In Search of Heresy.* But taken seriously and logically, the advice would put romanticism out of business and abolish tragedy. It is the kind of advice that most of us, whose lives are neither romantic nor tragic, are forced to give sooner or later—and to take. But there are some who are simply not like most of us, who cannot accept the human condition for what it is, who cannot resign themselves to the existence of injustice, ugliness, and pain —and who cannot accept the theological argument that suffering is a part of God's equation. One of those is Ivan Karamazov, who says: "If the suffering of children serves to complete the sum of suffering necessary for the acquisition of truth, I affirm from now onward that truth is not worth such a price." One may regard this attitude as childish, and futile, but it also contains the ultimate rebellion— against God. Huck Finn is perhaps a little closer to that rebellion than Holden; Huck can say, "All right, then I'll *go* to hell," but Holden has no hell to go to, at least no hell as specific as Huck's. It may seem preposterous to apply such terms as sanctity, even with due qualifications, to this prep-school fugitive. But to call him saintly is really no more of an exaggeration than to call him blind and cynical. If we must exaggerate, let us exaggerate in the right categories.

The refusal to accept the status quo in the universe marks not only adolescents; it also marks the saints and, at times, the mad. The connection is not accidental but necessary and functional. The young have the clarity and newness of vision, the relentless but two-dimensional logic, and the almost unbearable sensitivity that often characterize the saintly and the insane. A saint as well as a madman may be an adolescent who has refused to "grow up," who is unable or unwilling to cover his soul with the calluses necessary for the ordinary life, the crucial difference being that the saint finds a protective armor in religion while the madman's only protection is flight. All, in different ways, wage war with the-way-things-are; they are martyrs to the commonplace.

If Holden falls considerably short of heroic stature, it is because the author has, after all, limited his range and chosen to tell, in speech, setting, and incident, the story of an adolescent. The child or adolescent cannot be the hero of a tragedy because his powers are not fully developed and his defeat or destruction, no matter how affecting, is not as pitiful or terrible as the downfall of a human being at the height of his power and glory. But the fact remains that Holden Caulfield, if he is a rebel at all, is a rebel against the human condition and as such he deserves his small share of nobility.

In his essay *The Eye of Innocence* Leslie Fiedler ingeniously debunks the cult of the child and suggests that the Original Innocence we have come to worship in them is a reaction against Original Sin. The innocent child, in other words, is a myth like the noble savage—savage, perhaps, but not noble. Fiedler is particularly fascinating on this subject because by applying Freudian theory, he winds up standing solidly alongside the orthodox theologian. Using the insights of depth psychology (surely scientific and enlightened?) he reaches conclusions considerably closer to Saint Augustine or Calvin than to Freud. The orthodox theologian sees sin in the infant as well as in the adult; similarly the Freudian sees sex (which of course he does not call sin) in the infant as well as in the adult. With Original Sin replaced by the Original Id, Fiedler can gleefully reassert the demonic nature of the child. As he demolishes the liberals for their naïveté about the innocence of child witches, one can almost see him testifying at the trials in Salem. His essay suggests a new but as yet little noticed force at work—Freudian Puritanism.

Yet debunking "childism" does not, in the end, dispose of the child. It is surely no accident that in so many civilizations the child, like the fool, is assigned a special oracular authority. Nor can this be dismissed simply as superstition. It is part of mankind's collective experience that out of the mouths of the young can come truth and that in the eyes of the young the world is new—or, as Wordsworth put it, Youth is "Nature's Priest." All of Salinger's work is imbued with this belief, and it is only a matter of time before a Ph.D. candidate points out that in *A Perfect Day for Bananafish* Sybil is really a sybil. In cherishing the child, we cherish ourselves, or rather the memory of ourselves in youth. We hug what we once were, or think we were. But while it is true that we sentimentalize the child and innocence, surely we also sentimentalize age (particularly middle age) and experience. If some of us are overemotional about the dewy freshness of the half-grown, surely others are equally emotional about the dry, grown-up courage that it takes to live life as it is. Compromise can be sentimentalized as much as courage, and resignation has its own lyricism, the kind that Prufrock serves with tea and stale crumpets.

One pleasure, incidentally, of which both the sentimentalizers and the psychologizers of the child deprive us is a certain kind of humor, exemplified by the jolly sadism of Hilaire Belloc's *Cautionary Verses*. Both factions suspect our motives in laughing at those little boys eaten by lions and those little girls trapped in burning houses. Fiedler would be more in sympathy with this sort of humor than Salinger, but he would find behind the laughter all kinds of hate, cruelty, and perverted fantasies. For myself, I have long felt that Salinger's *Teddy* would have made a great little Belloc poem. Surely "Henry King, Who chewed bits of String, and was early cut off in Dreadful Agonies" and "George, Who played with a Dangerous Toy, and suffered a Catastrophe of considerable Dimensions" should welcome into their company "Teddy McArdle, Who had Strange Powers and was cut down to Size by his Sister." One can imagine the conclusion of the Belloc version:

. . . And then (oh Jealous Little Fool!)
His Sister pushed him in the Pool,
Succeeding with the first Attempt. He
Was not Surprised to find it Empty.
MORAL
Bright Little Boys who play with Zen
May not grow up to be Big Men.

Belloc would have done much better, of course. At any rate, *Cautionary Verses* is highly recommended after prolonged reading of either Salinger or Leslie Fiedler.

A part of the charge of immaturity often brought against Salinger is the fact that he does not deal with mature love. The implication is that he "escapes" from sex. It is an open question whether this escape is not one of the things that makes him so popular. The accepted formula for success on the best-seller lists is of course an abundance of sex, but it is entirely possible that a point of surfeit has been reached. "Mature love" between men and women has not always been at the center of the storytelling art. The great epics dealt more with the themes of war, nature, and the gods. The novel has made the love story so much a part of our very atmosphere that we can scarcely imagine it otherwise; but "mature love" alone has rarely been sufficient to sustain fiction, and it has nearly always needed the admixture of the other, older themes. It is just possible that Salinger's sexless story comes as something of a relief.

Alfred Kazin brings the charge of immaturity against Salinger's characters in a more specific and damaging way than other critics. He accuses the Glasses of being cute (Fiedler earlier used the same word about Huck), and by cuteness Kazin means a deliberate and calculated prolongation of adolescent winsomeness into adult life. With the adolescent, he feels, this winsomeness is a legitimate weapon against a world that is too much for him, but in the adult it becomes an unfair advantage. Furthermore he feels that the Glasses love only themselves and each other; for the rest of mankind, as Kazin puts it, there is only forgiveness, and the author is accused of abetting and blessing this cute little woolly nest of self-love by "his extraordinary cherishing" of the Glasses. John Updike, in the New York *Times*, raises a similar objection. Franny and Zooey and the other young Glasses, he feels, "condemn the world only to condescend to it, to forgive it." And he, too, feels that Salinger is their accomplice by cherishing them too exclusively: "Salinger loves the Glasses more than God loves them."

Quite a trick, of course, even for an author of Updike's considerable talent, to know just how much God loves the Glasses. What irritates Updike particularly is that Salinger not only loves his creatures but insists that the reader must love them too. He very shrewdly observes that "Salinger robs the reader of the initiative upon which love must be given." But the same could be said of Dickens. At any rate, it is likely that most readers are not so much irritated as exhilarated by the love which Salinger compels from them.

WITH THE GLASS FAMILY

Three passages from Franny and Zooey

She was wearing her usual at-home vesture—what her son Buddy (who was a writer, and consequently, as Kafka, no less, has told us, not a nice man) called her pre-notification-of-death uniform. It consisted mostly of a hoary midnight-blue Japanese kimono. She almost invariably wore it throughout the apartment during the day. With its many occultish-looking folds, it also served as the repository for the paraphernalia of a very heavy cigarette smoker and an amateur handyman; two oversized pockets had been added at the hips, and they usually contained two or three packs of cigarettes, several match folders, a screwdriver, a claw-end hammer, a Boy Scout knife that had once belonged to one of her sons, and an enamel faucet handle or two, plus an assortment of screws, nails, hinges, and ball-bearing casters—all of which tended to make Mrs. Glass chink faintly as she moved about in her large apartment.

"It's us," Zooey repeated, overriding her. "We're freaks, that's all. Those two bastards got us nice and early and made us into freaks with freakish standards, that's all. We're the Tattooed Lady, and we're never going to have a minute's peace, the rest of our lives, till everybody else is tattooed, too." More than a trifle grimly, he brought his cigar to his mouth and dragged on it, but it had gone out. "On top of everything else," he said immediately, "we've got 'Wise Child' complexes. We've never really got off the goddam air. Not one of us. We don't talk, we hold forth. We don't converse, we expound. At least I do. The minute I'm in a room with somebody who has the usual number of ears, I either turn into a goddam seer or a human hatpin. The Prince of Bores."

"It isn't just Wally. . . . It's everybody, I mean. Everything everybody does is so—I don't know—not wrong, or even mean, or even stupid necessarily. But just so tiny and meaningless and—sad-making. And the worst part is, if you go bohemian or something crazy like that, you're conforming just as much as everybody else, only in a different way." . . . [Franny] shook her head briefly, her face quite white, and for just a fractional moment she felt her forehead with her hand—less, it seemed, to find out whether she was perspiring than to check to see, as if she were her own parent, whether she had a fever. "I feel so funny," she said. "I think I'm going crazy. Maybe I'm already crazy."

To the receptive, he gives a sense of joy and *Gemütlichkeit* that is almost wholly absent from contemporary fiction. Perhaps only Dickens could provide a comparable sense of well-being, not only in his characters but in his treatment of life's humbler joys, notably food. Dickens's descriptions of the family gathered around the festive board evokes a cosmic coziness that resembles the extraordinary warmth generated in the sympathetic reader by the Glasses. The warmth is far less physical or sensuous; but precisely as one wants to be with the Dickens clan around the silver tureen, one longs to be part of a Glass family occasion—perhaps that extraordinary party where the junior vaudevillians put on their acts for Les and Bessie, or just going with Seymour to the barbershop down the street. David Leitch is right when he says, somewhat sarcastically, that the Glasses have been made to seem members of a "peculiarly intimate club, a club which Salinger readers are overtly invited to associate themselves with."

It is this clubbiness which provokes the objection that the Glasses love each other and themselves at the expense of others: the rest of the world is shut out. One does indeed get the feeling that there is an invisible barrier between the Glass living room and the rest of the universe. But what both Kazin and Updike do not fully acknowledge is that the Glass children themselves are very much aware of this. There is little the critics have said about them that they have not said about themselves.

The fact that, as Kazin charges, "they love certain people only" is surely known to Bessie when she accuses Zooey of being able to talk only to people he loves. When Zooey accuses himself and the others of being freaks, there is no reason to think that he does not mean it—or that Salinger does not mean it. Their cleverness, their cuteness, their sensitivity, irritates them quite as much as it irritates some critics: "If it makes them remarkable," says Arthur Mizener, "it is also a quite terrible burden [on themselves]." According to Kazin, the Glasses feel about society "that they are too sensitive to live in it." Perhaps the opposite is true; perhaps they are too sensitive to ignore it, to look the other way, to withdraw, as well-adjusted, busy, adult people withdraw into their protective shells when faced with society's terrors.

Like Holden, the Glasses simply cannot accept the injustices, the ugliness, the lovelessness, and the egomania that surround them. It is true that Holden and the Glasses dislike phonies too much, are too perturbed by all the people who are in Franny's words "so tiny and meaningless and sad-making." But that is, after all, the very condition which Zooey is trying to cure in his sister—and in himself. At the end of the story, after he has tried for hours to argue her out of her disgust with the world, he tells her the famous parable of the Fat Lady. It goes back to the time when the Glass children were quiz kids on a radio show and their wise, good, poetic, and revered brother Seymour made the youngsters shine their shoes before each performance, even though no one would see those shoes. It had to be done, said Seymour, for the Fat Lady—the incarnation of all the lonely, unlovable, unlovely people who presumably sat listening by their radios. And then Zooey drives home the point: "Are you listening to me? *There isn't anyone there who isn't Seymour's Fat Lady. . . . Don't you know that? Don't you know that goddam secret yet? And don't you know— listen to me, now—don't you know who that Fat Lady really is? . . .* Ah, buddy. Ah, buddy. It's Christ Himself. Christ Himself, buddy." With that, Franny is, apparently, appeased and goes serenely to sleep.

When I first read this story, I was carried along by the marvelous and heady stream of talk. These two characters did not precisely remind me of anyone I ever knew, because the Glasses are obviously not, and are not meant to be, realistic portrayals. But they did evoke a memory here, a recognition there, of the kind of overarticulate, overemotional young people who excitedly theorize about the universe and themselves, who forever question what they are saying and then question the question itself, who sound as if they knew it all (or felt it all), but who are vulnerable in their youth and lovable in their enthusiasm. When the Fat Lady made her first appearance, I winced. I could not help thinking for a few moments that this was parody, just as perhaps Zooey's admonition to his sister to "be God's actress" was parody, as well as the story of Christ dropping into the Glass kitchen and asking for some ginger ale. The parable of the Fat Lady was slightly repulsive and slightly too simple, and Salinger, as he often does, seemed to be daring one to take it or leave it.

What the friendly as well as the hostile critics have in common here is that they unhesitatingly attribute Zooey's views to Salinger; for the most part, they fail to see that Zooey's views *are in character*. The Glasses speak with perfect naturalness about someone having "a hell of a lot of kharma." They are both serious and not serious about religion; to them it is somewhere between toy and salvation. Zooey is not a prophet but an intelligent, engaging, rather glib, frighteningly articulate young television actor trying first this approach, then that, always with just a touch of the spiritual con man about him, to snap his sister out of a spiritual funk. Seen in that light, to repeat, the parable of the Fat Lady is in character; it is precisely what Zooey Glass would come up with. Salinger is much too close to his characters to permit any obvious hint of satire, but is there not between them and him just enough space for irony? He does not laugh at them, because he loves them; but he does smile at them—because he loves them. He indulges them, but he does not fail to judge them.

Perhaps Geismar feels something similar when in the Glass stories he finds a certain ambiguity, "where the artist both is and is not responsible for what he is saying." But to Geismar this ambiguity is a flaw, while actually it is the opening that admits the author's irony, his "joke" and his judgment. The ambiguity is strongest about Seymour, who is regarded by the surviving Glasses as something of a holy man. But there are hints in *Zooey* that coexistence with a saint, living or dead, can have its drawbacks and that Seymour's sainthood itself is open to question. Zooey senses quite clearly that Seymour has deformed them all, however lovingly, and that he has ultimately destroyed their peace through his suicide; why else would there be talk about having to forgive him? These hints of discord within the cozy Glass club become downright thunderous in *Seymour: An Introduction,* a story remarkably little discussed by critics and, one may guess, widely misunderstood.

It is generally assumed that the title means what it says and that this is a story about Seymour; but it is as much, if not more so, a story about the narrator, Buddy Glass. The story's overwhelming mannerisms, the convolutions, endless digressions and apologies, the narrator's asides to himself and to the reader, the ramblings toward and away from the subject, are usually dismissed as Salinger's self-indulgence of thought or sloppiness of style. But when Buddy Glass writes things like "with a striking resemblance to—alley oop —and myself," or "I live alone (but catless I'd like everybody to know)," or "I would to God the reader had something terrible to tell me first (O you out there—with your enviable golden silence)," or "I privately say to you, old friend (unto you, really, I'm afraid), please accept from me this unpretentious bouquet of very early blooming parentheses: (((()))))" or simply, in self-admonition: "(stop that now)"—Salinger is not speaking in his own voice but again *in character*. True, the style uncomfortably recalls Salinger's own self-consciousness in his jacket blurb to *Franny and Zooey* or in his rare, early magazine notes about himself; it sounds like a wild caricature of those things. But the story is an indirect character portrait of Buddy Glass. In one of those first-person narratives which Miss McCarthy dislikes, Salinger is letting us see and guess the personality of a weirdly, fantastically self-conscious and mannered writer on the point of breaking down under the strain of living with Seymour's ghost.

There are hints not only that it was always difficult to live with the near-saintly Seymour but also that his saintliness as well as his talent may have been exaggerated by his family. Along with genuine love for the dead man there are hints of envy and of terror. When Buddy exclaims, "Why does this exhaust me so? The hands are sweating, the bowels churning?" or "This last little pentimento, or whatever it is, has started me sweating literally from head to foot," Salinger is forcing us to witness a crack-up far more severe than Franny's, and motivated far less simply. He is showing us that the members of the Glass club may be paying a high price for that cozy withdrawal from the world, that refuge which earlier had seemed so enviable and, to some, so cute.

THE FLOW OF LIFE

Two instants from Nine Stories

The swinging door opened from the dining room and Boo Boo Tannenbaum, the lady of the house, came into the kitchen. She was a small, almost hipless girl of twenty-five, with styleless, colorless, brittle hair pushed back behind her ears, which were very large. She was dressed in knee-length jeans, a black turtleneck pullover, and socks and loafers. Her joke of a name aside, her general unprettiness aside, she was—in terms of permanently memorable, immoderately perceptive, small-area faces—a stunning and final girl. She went directly to the refrigerator and opened it. As she peered inside, with her legs apart and her hands on her knees, she whistled, unmelodically, through her teeth, keeping time with a little uninhibited, pendulum action of her rear end. Sandra and Mrs. Snell were silent. . . .

"Sandra . . ."

"Yes, Ma'am?" Sandra looked alertly past Mrs. Snell's hat.

"Aren't there any more pickles? I want to bring him a pickle."

"He et 'em," Sandra reported intelligently. "He et 'em before he went to bed last night"
          —from "Down at the Dinghy"

I remember a significant incident that occurred just a day or two after Bobby and I arrived in New York. I was standing up in a very crowded Lexington Avenue bus, holding on to the enamel pole near the driver's seat, buttocks to buttocks with the chap behind me. For a number of blocks the driver had repeatedly given those of us bunched up near the front door a curt order to "step to the rear of the vehicle." Some of us had tried to oblige him. Some of us hadn't. At length, with a red light in his favor, the harrassed man swung around in his seat and looked up at me, just behind him. At nineteen, I was a hatless type, with a flat, black, not particularly clean, Continental-type pompadour over a badly broken-out inch of forehead. He addressed me in a lowered, an almost prudent tone of voice. "All right, buddy," he said, "let's move that ass." It was the "buddy," I think, that did it. Without even bothering to bend over a little—that is, to keep the conversation at least as private, as de bon goût, as he'd kept it—I informed him, in French, that he was a rude, stupid, overbearing imbecile, and that he'd never know how much I detested him. Then, rather elated, I stepped to the rear of the vehicle.—from "De Daumier-Smith's Blue Period"

The method of the telling is admittedly devious. The author plays games with the reader and with reality when he makes Buddy Glass sound like the author of *The Catcher in the Rye* and makes Buddy the butt of the familiar rumors (the Buddhist monastery, the sanatorium) that from time to time have circulated about J. D. Salinger. All this may be an irritating private joke, but it also has a literary purpose. In theatrical terms Salinger is trying to destroy the proscenium. Like a number of playwrights from Pirandello to Jack Gelber, he is attempting to bring the audience completely into the action, to make them forget what is real and what is not. The same is true of the rambling, fussy style, the neurotic asides, the clinical notes, that ooze from the narrator. It may be argued that this method does not work or that it is not worth the effort, but it should at least be recognized that it *is* a method and not merely self-indulgence and sloppiness. I, for one, feel that the method works hair-raisingly well, though it should not and could not be attempted often, and that *Seymour* is Salinger's most impressive story. The case could hardly be put better than it has been by John Updike who, despite serious objections to Salinger's manner and technique, says: "The willingness to risk excess on behalf of one's obsessions is what distinguishes artists from entertainers." One might add, for Updike, that the willingness to recognize the fact is what distinguishes critics from reviewers.

In a curious way the convulsions of *Seymour*, the carefully built-up struggle between Salinger-Buddy and the subject matter, recall that old literary theme, The Revolt of the Puppets. If the story is a form of ventriloquism, the dummy seems to be taking over—recalling Cavalcanti's film *Dead of Night*, in which the ventriloquist, played by Michael Redgrave, was engaged in a schizoid and deadly struggle with the painted, wooden figure he used in his act and which gradually became a hostile incarnation of his own other self. Whether any of this reflects real problems the real Salinger may be having with his series about the Glasses is not known and is perhaps beside the point. As a work of fiction, *Seymour* is fascinating partly because it suggests a struggle on the edge of sanity, a rebellion of puppet against puppeteer.

American literary criticism, in George Steiner's phrase, is a great machine constantly in need of raw material. It is, in fact, many machines; press the right button, pull the right lever, and off the conveyor belt will roll social consciousness, depth psychology, historical perspective, neatly stamped-out pedantry and, gratifyingly often, passion for literature. It is possible, as has been charged, that in this vast enterprise Salinger's importance has been overrated. But this concern seems already out of date. There are signs that the critics, far from overestimating Salinger, have begun to turn against him. It seems "in" these days to be anti-Salinger.

To this must be added Salinger's personal inaccessibility, his total refusal to communicate with anyone in the world outside his family and close friends; if one resents the Glasses' fictional withdrawal from the world, one is likely to resent their creator's actual withdrawal even more. If there is a club centering around the Glasses, there is an even more exclusive club centering around Salinger himself, and it is considerably harder to join it than, say, the Union. J. D. Salinger's isolation from the world is a unique accomplishment in American life. He certainly is "the boy / who can enjoy / invisibility," and he enjoys it with more grim determination than anyone else who is not confined in a high-security prison or a monastery of the strictest rule.

But the feat is not universally applauded. One critic angrily calls Salinger's attitude an affectation, and another refers to him as the Greta Garbo of American letters. One of his early editors feels that a writer is a public person, no more entitled to privacy than a legislator. The point is debatable, but there is no doubt that Salinger's elusiveness adds a special element to his fiction. He plays with it, and on it. He works unmistakable facts about himself into his stories, and grins at the resulting confusion when in his jacket notes to *Franny and Zooey* he refers to Buddy Glass as his "alter-ego and collaborator." In short, he teases. What is all the more remarkable is that Salinger, who has never talked back to the critics, apparently follows them carefully. It seems incredible, but all the elaborate effort to withdraw has not really allowed him to shut out the world. A popular monthly not long ago decided to publish some material about Salinger. Representations were made, and the magazine dropped the project. The reason given was that anything appearing in print about Salinger slows him down for weeks and even months. There is a spy hole in the wall. He is not seen, but he sees.

Yet all of this—the critical machine's hunger for raw material, the reaction produced by Salinger's popular success, the irritation caused by his elaborate elusiveness—will not fully account for the critical attitudes toward Salinger. He apparently touches something very deep in us. If some dwell a little too emphatically on Holden's sainthood or Salinger's knighthood, it must be because we are so badly in need of saints and knights. If others grow a little shrill about the Glasses' anti-social traits and the intellectual softness of their religion, it must be because we feel the need for a powerful community and strong, clear ideas.

Salinger's extraordinary, perhaps unrivaled popularity with the younger generation has been attributed to the fact that he writes about it, that he speaks its language, and that, in *The Catcher in The Rye* at least, he expresses its discontents. Let down by World War II and its aftermath, accustomed to the Cold War, shaken by the Bomb—though probably not nearly as much as it is often suggested—the young distrust utopias and have withdrawn into a system of morality that is largely private and small-scale. At its heart is that hatred of the "phony" which Holden personifies. (It is interesting to note that the condemnation of the phony is essentially negative. The term itself has no exact contrary; *wrong* has *right*, *square* has *hip*, *out* has *in*, but *phony*—bypassing *sincere, true,* and *real*, none of which quite fits—has only the awkward and vague *non-phony* as its affirmative opposite.)

This atmosphere inevitably recalls the era of nineteenth-century romanticism; then, too, the promise of utopia disappeared in blood, leaving the younger generation disillusioned and ready to escape into the personal search for truth and beauty. But despite their incessant sentimentality about death, the nineteenth century's young romantics were more vigorous, more eccentric, more public in their yearnings than their present counterparts; nowadays Byron going forth to fight in Greece might still be applauded, with some reservations, but his drinking wine from a skull would certainly be dismissed as phony. Thus American youth today may be neoromantic, but it enjoys a more private, more limited romanticism, more given to the small gesture than to great adventure, more tending to introspection than to the dream. In a sense Salinger fits that mood.

But the mood is not wholly new. The American young have always been more sheltered than those of other civilizations and certainly less concerned with politics. For centuries the European student has taken his place on the barricades. To this day "student riots" are a familiar and significant factor in European politics. The phenomenon has no equivalent in the United States. With all due oversimplification, it might be said that in Europe revolutions are made by the young, in America by the middle-aged.

The revolutionary political and social literature of the twenties and thirties was in part written by young men, but it was not really treasured by youth. The writers who stirred young readers were always the romantics, the nonsocial, nonpolitical ones from Cooper to Hemingway to Fitzgerald. After decades of the political, the social, and the psychological novel, the young could only feel relief when they met Salinger. His adventures may be small, his battles all interior, but the gleam of delight in his eye is unmistakable. It is the gleam of a romantic.

"Delight" is not a proper critical term, but delight is what Salinger has to offer the halfway sympathetic reader, including the young. Martin Green, in his recent book *A Mirror for Anglo-Saxons*, remarks that Salinger is not so much a writer who depicts life as one who celebrates it. This is an accurate characterization of the humor and the love in his work, if not of the darker patches in *Seymour*. Ultimately the most serious charge against him is that his output is too small, that his Songs of Innocence do not reach us often enough. What we need is more Salinger fiction, not to feed that critical machine, but to start a few more celebrations.

Henry Anatole Grunwald is a senior editor of Time. *This essay will introduce an anthology of Salinger criticism to be published in June by Harper and Brothers.*

Siné by the Sea

. . . *for those who can't swim*

. . . *in Australia*   . . . *at Bi-arritz*   . . . *on the Riviera*   . . . *in Algeria*

What to wear on the beach is one of those questions that transcends national boundaries. Maurice Siné's nationality is French. Creator of a book of punning drawings entitled *The French Cat,* in its American edition, and cartoonist for the Paris newspaper *L'Express,* he is best known for the biting ridicule and laughter—quintessentially Parisian—with which he belabors his country's politicians, priests, policemen, and paratroopers. But his suggestions for swimming attire are drawn in an international language that will be intelligible anywhere. They have appeared in Paris in the collection *Siné dessins de l'Express (parus et non parus),* published by J.-J. Pauvert.

| . . . in Germany | . . . at Deauville | . . . in England | . . . in Mexico |

THEATRE

The Hunt for Heroes

Our generation, at least in the non-Communist world, is in difficulties about its heroes. Heroism, understood as courage in action, we can still recognize and applaud; but the individual hero, defined as the personification of what the age intends to be, has become a wraith. Heroes will not thrive in every moral climate; today they do not seem to thrive even in England—after Greece their natural habitat. But English writers are still out hero hunting, a proposition that can be demonstrated by three plays from London which have endowed the current Broadway season with such distinction as it has had. The quarry that they have brought home is another matter.

Robert Bolt, author of *A Man for All Seasons,* went seeking one hero and came up with another. His subject is Sir Thomas More, and he celebrates this noble, wise, and beautiful man in a play of such elegance as we now rarely see. Its speech (which is not infrequently the speech of More himself) flows with the smooth strength of fine cloth; its machinery is ingenious to the point of wit; it is concerned with lofty and universal issues. And it is performed by the large Anglo-American company—and especially by Paul Sco-

field in the title role—in a style of crystal sharpness and sparkle. This company makes of acting not only an art but the most enticing of sports. I cannot imagine a more appetizing theatrical occasion.

The playwright believes that the magnetism of an absolute principle is what gives life meaning and flavor, and is at pains to demonstrate the accessible humanity of his subject. More, who moves in Scofield's conception with the bent shoulders of a scholar and the reaching stride of a Crusader, is a wit and a gourmet, a man readily amused by folly, delighting in the duel of intelligence, immersed in love—for his wife and daughter, for his sporting friend the Duke of Norfolk, for his king, and for his valet. And immersed most deeply of all in love for his God.

At the moment when he is a pivot to the conscience of the Christian world, More is a man at ease. He is probably the most reasonable man of his age, but it is an age when reason and faith can be synonymous. More understands the ways of men and states; more pertinently, he understands young Henry VIII. He knows that Queen Catherine will be put aside and Anne Boleyn will achieve the throne; he appreciates the reasons of state and of passion that will

make this inevitable, the scholastic argument that will make it palatable. But the Pope has set his hand against the deed, and the Pope speaks with the voice of God. To flout that voice is heresy, and heresy is folly. More cannot be moved from his stand because he cannot be made to take leave of his own reason. He is thus a man at ease.

To our eyes he is also a man in a frame: he could have been painted by Memling. Bolt conceives him as perfection made animate. There is not much room for movement in that concept, and movement is the genius of the theatre. Furthermore, movement is the substance of our society. We are defined, not by our creeds, but by our orbits; our science is a system of relative truths, our souls are the sums of warring impulses. So to say of a character that he is perfectly good is as estranging as if one were to say that he is completely mad. We cannot relate to such men. I find in retrospect that the More of this play has turned as still as a tapestry; another figure beckons to me as hero.

This one is carried on the program as The Common Man. As played by George Rose, he is the evident crony of Shakespeare's citizens of the town; he would have torn Cinna for his verses and urged the crown on Richard III. He is variously employed in the play as More's valet, a boatman, a spy, a tapster, a jailor, and ultimately as More's headsman. He is also the interlocutor, reading out bits of history, explaining where we now find ourselves, whisking properties and bits of costume about to change scenes. Bolt uses this character with marvelous dexterity to lend crispness and speed to his pageantry and to season his solemn deliberations with shrewd digs in the ribs. Bolt, an aristocrat, adorns his palace of the mind with a gargoyle, but invites us to remember who we are and disown the fellow.

Alas, we cannot. For Bolt's gargoyle is a surviving sort of man, and that is what we are—a surviving sort of men. The lyric grace of *A Man for All Seasons*, the banners and bugles of its testimony to God's truth, are beauties that fade with poignant speed. What remains strong and warm in the mind is the ape at Sir Thomas's elbow, the antic opportunist who claims no more for himself than that his humanity is a persistent germ on the earth. It is a bitter

kernel within the rich fruit of humane and elegant poetry, and not the point intended. But adoration does not make heroes; recognition is what counts.

That being the case, we should find a hero in the wounded, neurotic, self-besotted man known variously as Ross, Shaw, and Lawrence of Arabia. If More was the hero as perfection, Lawrence was the hero as enigma; that should be more in our style. But Terence Rattigan, whose *Ross* is a dramatization of the desert warrior's glory and eclipse, is not the writer to reveal him. Rattigan deals in another kind of perfection —perfect theatre. For him, reality, morality, beauty, are whatever plays. I do not mean that rudely, as an accusation of dishonesty. We all perceive selectively, and the more expert a man becomes at his trade, the greater danger he runs that his trade will filter his perceptions. It is almost certain to happen to artists who offer the world their crafts and withhold themselves. Rattigan knows a human life in acts and curtain lines.

Ross is a consistently absorbing and seriously motivated play; it contains all

of Lawrence that the playwright could discern, and that is quite a lot. But the character lacks the overtones that might suggest where his life extended beyond the frame of this particular stage. Rattigan's Lawrence is as overt as a marionette and, once the curtain is down, he stores as conveniently.

That is true generally of Rattigan's characters, and in part it is what makes them so vivid. He can construct a sergeant major with a heart of gold, or a scholar-warrior like General Allenby, who is as complete and satisfying as an egg. Such characters are realer than life because they have no unprojectable, private dimension to blur them. That may do very well for the supernumeraries, but if your purpose is to bring a complex man like Lawrence into communion with your audience, it will not prove sufficient. A Lawrence complete on stage is no more meaningful than a Hamlet complete on stage. And a play that does not allow for intuition cannot be tragedy, can scarcely be a drama. It may be—and in this case certainly is— engrossing entertainment.

Two dramatic heroes and an "anti-hero" from Britain established themselves last season on Broadway. From left to right: Sir Thomas More (Paul Scofield), T. E. Lawrence, alias Ross (John Mills), and Mac Davies the Caretaker (Donald Pleasence).

Glen Byam Shaw, who directed *Ross*, and John Mills, who plays the title role, are in such rapport with Rattigan that they underscore his limitations. Mills's characterization is a series of tableaux in which, one by one, he mimes the facets of this notoriously many-faceted man. He enters in turn as the boyish romantic, the fanatic ascetic, the cocky nonconformist, the grieving father of his troops, the tortured animal, the humble penitent, the genius hiding behind an R.A.F. serial number. Each "impression" of Lawrence is instantly recognizable and theatrically interesting; no one, presumably, is supposed to ask whether he was a man or a string of beads. I enjoyed this bravura work, but Lawrence's candidacy for the hero's laurel will have to wait for a more encompassing, less Procrustean advocate.

Messrs. Bolt and Rattigan, in their very different ways, approach the hero by way of legend. The approach of Harold Pinter in *The Caretaker* is by way of allegory. The instant Donald Pleasence, as Mac Davies, alias Bernard Jenkins—stubble-cheeked, mean-eyed, and swaddled in rags—steps into view, one recognizes a popular spokesman of our day: the anti-hero. A hero may be a creature of history or of fiction, but in either case he can be real. An anti-hero, however, is by nature a thing of myth, a philosophical concept arrived at by reversing all the signs of heroism and drawing a graph of the result. The "real" opposite of a hero is a villain; an anti-hero is a construct, a conception peculiarly appropriate to an age that discovered the neutrino, a particle of matter that has no mass and carries no electrical charge, is therefore undetectable, but must exist because it permits certain calculations to balance. We have our own kind of faith, and the anti-hero has his own kind of reality.

On a factual level *The Caretaker* recites a brief and melancholy episode in the life of a bum who knows his rights. Davies has been fired from his job as dishwasher in a cheap café, as the result of kicking up a row, and has been brought to a derelict house somewhere in West London by Aston, who looks out for the place for Mick, the owner and his younger brother. Aston gives the old man a bed, some shoes, a few shillings—for which he gets small thanks and no gratitude. They talk in each other's presence; but since neither attends, they cannot be said to converse. This exasperates Davies, who wants charity, but still more wants to be noticed. Aston is as dispassionate as a board (his brain, it turns out, has been hobbled by electro-therapy).

Mick, who pops in and out unpredictably, gives Davies no charity but a great deal of attention. He threatens him, flatters him, schemes with him, calls him friend. The job of caretaker seems to be in the offing. The old man is alternately terrified and tickled pink. But what with the impassivity of his benefactor and the instability of his friend, what with his immunity to kindness and defenselessness against daydreaming, Davies is edged into a tighter and tighter corner of the rubbish-laden room. Until suddenly the brothers revile him for a stinking nuisance and throw him the hell out of the place. Curtain.

This is performed with a brilliance I should be quite at a loss to recapture on paper. The effectiveness of Pinter's prose is not only in its spare precision, but in its aching pauses and jumbled profusion of secondhand ideas and inapplicable observations. It is the language of men caught in the plumbing of society, scraps in the sink trap. And the three actors sustain the suspended action with a pretense to reason and purpose that is, quite literally, hideously funny. Pleasence's accent is an insult to sound, his face is a social blight. He gestures with an expansive vacuity that catches exactly the blind feelers of the stupid conniver. It is beautiful work. Aston (Robert Shaw) is large, pale, and saltless. He is that modern remittance man, the fellow who lives somehow on welfare. He has a screwdriver and a tin of small parts, and he "fixes" things. He is turned off. His brother is a more active modern type: the kind who has it made—someday. Uneducated, undisciplined, deceived by the egalitarianism of the times into thinking himself as good as anyone else, he has no skill but lingo (Mick can talk décor like a Mayfair interior decorator). He wears a leather jacket and tight trousers.

There is electricity, certainly, in the unsparing accuracy with which Pinter catches these three casualties of our abundant age (I wish, though, that I understood why he inflicts brain surgery on Aston: it seems to make him an accident rather than a casualty). But the reporting is not the limit of the excitement. *The Caretaker* is allegory, as it would have to be with an anti-hero at its axis. I don't approve of translating allegory; it is like explaining jokes. But in a sketchy way, the older brother behaves rather like destiny, existence, what we used to call God—doling out impassively the things a man needs to go on breathing. He is never exactly present, but he is around. The younger brother—popping in and out, always ready with a smile or a kick in the teeth, handsome, and flashy—could be taken to represent luck, what a man cosies up to at his desperate peril. And the old man—appointed caretaker (at an unspecified fee and with undefined duties) of a cluttered and decaying room surrounded by a planetary system of empty, unfinished, and forbidden rooms; kicking at fate and flirting with luck and flung at last into oblivion by the two of them—this Mac Davies of the itching garments and blindly working mouth bears a grisly resemblance to the whole pack of us. Mr. Pinter is no optimist, and the hero he offers us is a joke in questionable taste. But he is, after all, a playwright and not a magician (though his skill has touches of magic). A hero is the image of itself that the age projects, what it intends to be. According to Mr. Pinter, we project Mac Davies; Samuel Beckett calls him Molloy or Krapp, Edward Albee calls him the American Dream, Eugene Ionesco calls him a rhinoceros. Can all these playwrights be talking about us? It grows chilly.   ROBERT HATCH

BOOKS

Paris at Five O'Clock

A year or two ago several of my friends told me I ought to read a remarkable French author who was writing "experimental novels" of great interest and originality: Claude Mauriac, son of the austere and eminent François Mauriac. They mentioned in particular a book about a dinner party, in which there was no narrator and no continuous thread of "story": the entire work was a sixteen-part fugue composed of the interlocking conversations and private thoughts of the host and hostess and their six guests. This sounded clever but trivial; I detest formal dinner parties anyhow: I made no effort to procure the book. Yet I remembered it, promising myself that, if I ever had a little leisure, I should read it.

Then, last winter, I heard that Claude Mauriac had published another novel, with the curious title *La marquise sortit à cinq heures* (to be issued in English by George Braziller this spring as, literally enough, *The Marquise Went Out at Five*). Some readers may recognize the source of the title. Paul Valéry, asked why he never embarked on a novel, said "I could not bear to write down the words 'The Marquise went out at five.'" A poet, Valéry detested logical sequences and obvious patterns. He meant that he could not endure the boredom that too many novelists inflict both on themselves and on their patient readers: the tedium of telling a story in its straight chronological order ("Next morning at exactly eleven o'clock Raskolnikov went into the police station") and with every detail painstakingly invented and particularized, nothing, however trivial, left to the reader's imagination ("Porphyry's office was a room neither large nor small,

containing a large writing desk, a bureau, a bookcase, and several chairs"). Only an interesting writer would choose such a lively title. Perhaps Claude Mauriac was more than a batik designer: he might have something to say.

I bought the French edition of *La marquise sortit à cinq heures*, published by Albin Michel, and started to read it. After an hour or so I decided it was interesting but unintelligible—or rather, like *Finnegans Wake*, comprehensible only to those who were willing to spend several months or years cracking the code. No characters are directly introduced or named. There are no direct indications of place and time, except a little inserted map of a quarter on the Left Bank in Paris. There are no chapter divisions: the book is a continuous flow of three hundred pages of prose. No, not continuous, except as a stream running through rapids is continuous; and not ordinary prose, but rather a succession of fragmentary thoughts, broken conversations, echoes of speech and song, as varied and mutable as the bubbles and swirls and foam of that mountain stream. The first three paragraphs are introduced by the favorite French typographical device for showing incompleteness, three dots:

. . . De l'autre côté du carrefour

and the same three dots terminate each of them. Evidently these are sections of the interior monologues of different people. But then come three utterances, each introduced by a dash:

— Alors Chiffonnette, elle prit le cartable . . .

Apparently these are words spoken aloud, although we are not told who speaks them. By working carefully over

the text, one can begin to identify the speakers and the thinkers. But even this is not easy. On the second page the same person first speaks—with an introductory dash—and then reflects . . . with an introductory triple dot. Just as we begin to divine who these people are (a mysterious marquise and two lonely men meditating, a little girl talking to her mother and her mother thinking while the child prattles), two new speakers intervene. They disappear in their turn. More thoughts of the marquise, the men, the mother. More conversation; new speakers; the thoughts of other strangers; and so, for page upon page, on and on. It is like being blindfolded and set down in a strange city and told to find one's way without asking questions, merely by listening to the multifarious sounds and voices that, at many different levels of intensity and intelligibility, assail one's ears. To read such a novel at a normal pace is quite impossible. So I concluded, and abandoned *The Marquise Went Out at Five*.

Yet I felt guilty. Perhaps it was worth a further effort. There were some charming things in it: the crazy marquise, the child's story about Chiffonnette and Bigaudis, and the personality of Paris, that lewd, elegant, vivacious city, emerging behind all the talk . . .

I turned to Mauriac's earlier novel, *The Dinner Party*.* This is far shorter and far easier. The host and hostess with their guests are named on the seating plan and soon identify themselves by their exchanges of conversation and their thoughts about one another. Although this novel also is a continuous, chapterless flow, it is clearly punctuated by the rhythm that everyone knows. On the first page, the guests are being

* *Le dîner en ville*, Albin Michel, Paris, 1959; English translation by Merloyd Lawrence, published by Braziller, New York, 1960.

Alone in Company

Typifying Claude Mauriac's technique, four characters soliloquize (perhaps simultaneously) in his The Dinner Party, *a novel that begins and ends one evening around a Paris table:*

The old lady:

. . . Little Jérôme Aygulf is a polite, well-behaved child. Even if he does pick his nose. When the Meilleuses lived here they had none of these antique mirrors. There was a Van Gogh, hanging on a background of yellow silk, lit indirectly to bring out the gleaming orange and dazzling greens. They had to sell it, along with everything else, before they died alone and penniless, within a few months of each other. The fear of losing the little I have, as my income shrinks and shrinks, and of dying alone and penniless. And an invalid, why not? A broken hip, at the very least. I must be careful going downstairs tonight. As I lean over, the reflections move along the three prongs of my fork. On the decanters, teardrops of light . . .

The producer's wife:

. . . That letter to my landlady will be so difficult I must write it tomorrow and tell her dear madam no madam you have no right to keep me from installing an antenna on the roof there is a law no I can put it better than that madam in answer to your letter of the permit me to draw your attention to such and such a clause in the code regulating the use of Léon-Pierre told me which law it was but it still doesn't sound right what a chore writing this letter my whole Sunday will be ruined *my whole life ruined lost it is not fair to have to die it's horrible I am so afraid how can they sit there and not be shrieking with horror* . . .

The screen writer:

. . . It has been so long since I have written anything, except the scenarios which I write for a living and which are not bad as stories go; the films made from them are at least controversial. But after all! Mallarmé himself only wrote three poems during one twenty-year period of his life. Again that anguish. His works lasted. They exist today. But mine! It is not too late. The next time I find myself between films I will work on something other than a scenario. I will write a book. Like those I wrote between the ages of eighteen and twenty-eight. Novels which almost no one ever read. Which I never dared to re-read. But in which the undeniable talent revealed in my screenplays was already demonstrated, without being obscured by the compromises, the falsification, and the deception necessary to the screen. I am a success. I have made a name for myself. But in the movies, and that does not count . . .

The nervous millionaire:

. . . Rich as I am, and good-looking, although a bit (a very little bit) too stout, I could find happiness in the arms of a chambermaid. (Oh, how happy I could be!) Perspiring already. (One of my difficulties.) (Not the only one.) (Alas!) Try to wipe your forehead without being noticed. It is not because I am worried (What could I be afraid of?) that I am perspiring; it is just that I am too warm. This room is unbearably hot. (But why this panic?) . . .

seated. On the last, they have risen and are passing into the drawing room. Between these termini the courses succeed one another, the wine is poured and repoured, and both the conversation and the thoughts of the eight characters become (as in many dinner parties) more intense and indiscreet. At the opening we know nothing of these people but their names. By the close, having heard their talk and overheard their meditations, we know them well: we have seen much of their past, and we can forecast their future (see excerpts at left).

Encouraged by the brilliance and clarity of this novel, I turned back again to *The Marquise*. Reading much more slowly, lingering on each monologue or conversation until I had identified the characters concerned, and writing out a list of their names and backgrounds, I found that, like figures on a photograph in the developing tank, they grew clear, separated themselves from one another, acquired lights and shadows and individual poses and characteristic expressions. Meanwhile, the shape of the book in time, and its internal punctuation, also emerged. It is a fine conception, worked out with a skill that few novelists have the patience or the delicacy to apply.

The novel tells the story of one hour in one spot near the center of Paris. It begins at five P.M. on a hot summer day and ends, after a welcome thundershower, just as six o'clock strikes. The characters are nearly all Parisians. Some live near the Carrefour de Buci —it is a real place, just off the Boulevard St. Germain, on the way to the Seine and the Pont Neuf. Others merely pass through it. Scores of lives cross one another at this crossroads and this hour. Listening to their voices, we distinguish four different types.

Some are quiet folk leading their ordinary lives: the policeman, controlling six streams of traffic and feeling the heat; the old man selling vegetables and fruit from a barrow; Monsieur Taconnet, the businessman, and his typist ("Can I get the letters all out by 5:30?"). Some, as in every big city, are passing through with interests elsewhere. A pretty redhead with blue slacks and a white blouse and no brassière runs fast and dodges traffic and dives into the subway and leaves a broad wake of emotion behind her. A male extrovert in a Ferrari waits growling for the policeman's whistle TRIIIT and then takes off AHHAHA round the *carrefour* "Circle of Terror" VROOAPP. VROOP. ROOAAR. Detectives staked out to watch for a criminal who has a date with an accomplice here, between five and six, loiter in nonchalant silence.

Others, again, are in the grip of crisis. A quiet little maniac believes that electrical waves from all the transmitters in France are concentrating on him; he is also obsessed by small children and thinks often of his niece Lucette ("Why won't my brother trust me with her?"). Old Monsieur Loubert tells a friend how his wife, "after fifty-five years of happiness, in the same bed," died and left him alone. Lucien makes love to Minouche in a hotel room; and then, with her debased and conscient complicity, makes love to Ida, the maid next door. These are "transients," but each carries within him, ticking, a cargo of frightful, explosive power.

The central characters of the book are in view or in thought from the beginning to the end. The rich and sensual author Bertrand Carnéjoux (so called, no doubt, because he likes to toy with flesh) has broken up his marriage and is living alone, thinking out a new novel. As the book opens, his young wife Martine has just left his apartment, after bringing their daughter Rachel, aged four, to see him on a duty visit. (Little Rachel, who says at the end of a long walk that she is *fafiguée,* is one of the most delightful children I have ever met in fiction.) Carnéjoux was also one of the chief figures in *The Dinner Party,* where we saw that he had three mistresses simultaneously, one being the maid who helped to serve dinner. Now he is alone and, for the moment, free of all obsessions except literature. The schoolboy Patrice Reslaut is tortured by ideal love for a schoolgirl, Valérie, and by base

lust for the anonymous nudes of peep shows, and by jealousy of a rival whom Valérie seems to like equally well—or better? The quiet merchant of autographs and old books, watching the rolling traffic of the Carrefour de Buci, lets his mind rove back over the history of Paris, which, like a rich wine, acquires greater strength and beauty with the passing years. And the marquise? Who is the marquise who went out at five, talking to herself, lamenting her middle-aged spread, and still cruising up and down the streets at six? She is not a lady, but an old male homosexual called Zerbarian—one of Mauriac's funniest characters, comic most of all in his fat frustration.

The chief technical problem in writing a book like this is that it contains no single "plot." It has, in Mauriac's words, "unity of place, unity of time, multiplicity of action." However, he has contrived to give it something like a unity of action: partly by reporting activities that are similar, activities of the early evening, people going home, looking for love and rest, reflecting on the past day; partly by interweaving, in the mind of the antiquarian Desprez, stage after stage in the history of this quarter of Paris with this present hour which is already passing into history; and partly—this is subtle—by projecting the whole moving spectacle on the mind of Carnéjoux the novelist, so that it becomes at once the world he observes, the novel he is preparing to write, and the novel we are reading.

This is a truly modern work. Even its models are all new. It is like a highly intelligent film made by a mobile camera and then edited, with many flashbacks and much crosscutting, by a poetic producer. It is like an on-the-spot tape recording; indeed, it could well be made into a play for radio, with dozens of different voices rising and fading against the busy background music of a city. In literature one of its models is *Ulysses,* which within one twenty-four hour period gives us the life of a city, with many interior monologues, many fragmentary sounds and speeches over-

heard, and much of that indescribable half-comic poetry that exudes from the life of common folk. (*The Marquise* ends with a big rhapsody reminiscent in shape of Molly Bloom's final reverie.) Eliot's *Waste Land,* blending past and present, vulgarity and nobility, the imagined and the reminiscent and the overheard, is another work in this style.

Like other practitioners of "the new novel" in France (as analyzed by Richard Gilman in the January, 1962, HORIZON), Mauriac has given up the artificial concept of a single thread of plot called "the story"; and like them, he brings the reader into direct and intimate confrontation with his characters. Jules Romains, too, is one of Mauriac's masters. In *Men of Good Will* he evoked the collective life of the city of Paris; and the episodic contrapuntal plan of that enormous work is adapted to *The Marquise,* although on a smaller, far more concentrated scale. Romains's doctrine of "unanimism"—which makes a street full of people or a small group of friends capable of becoming a higher, although less durable, entity than the individuals that compose it—is beautifully expressed in the life of the Carrefour de Buci. Whether Mauriac also knows Durrell's Alexandria quartet I cannot say: the two men are much of an age and have clearly been working along similar lines.

But any novelist's work, however ingenious its technique and however distinguished its models, will be arid and unrewarding unless he can create people, make them act naturally and surprisingly, let us hear their voices and see their movements, so that they appear to us, not puppets on strings or actors on celluloid, but flesh and blood and spirit like ourselves. As I finished *The Marquise Went Out at Five,* I forgot that I was reading a book and felt as though I were standing on a balcony above the Carrefour de Buci, sharing for an hour the life of those gay, harassed, volatile, intelligent, sensual, xenophobic people of Paris, who are the real hero of Mauriac's eloquent and penetrating novel.   GILBERT HIGHET

MOVIES

Not By the Book

Seeing a pleasant, innocuous movie and later hearing someone "who has read the novel" pick it to pieces, is a somewhat tiring experience. Film makers get indignant about such procedures and protest that movies should be judged on their own merits, and never mind where the original ideas came from. They have a point, and the few serious film critics writing for the New York dailies usually avoid comparison between film and book (the unserious ones don't read books). Having said this, I should like to indulge in a comparison—between Allen Drury's novel *Advise and Consent* and the film treatment of it recently made by Otto Preminger.*

I remember, after seeing Walt Disney's *Treasure Island,* how I reread the novel and found—sacrilegious as it may sound—that the changes made in Stevenson's story gave the plot more tightness and logic. This was, of course, an atypical discovery. More frequently a novel is hanged, drawn, quartered, and its bowels torn out, in order that its story may fit comfortably into the never-never land of American movies. The borders of this mysterious country are defined by "what the public wants" and what the Motion Picture Code allows, and within its realm love's problems do not begin but end with marriage; the honest man's answer to provocation is a punch in the nose; and girls take their dresses off in men's apartments only when they have been caught in the rain (but they remain chaste).

Europe does better at times, but not always. After Somerset Maugham's three-story movie *Trio* appeared, a British publisher brought out a book that included both the screenplays of the three stories and the originals them-

* For a glimpse of Preminger in another role, see page 81.

Otto Preminger

selves; it was a hair-raising demonstration of how in each case the essence of the story, its point and wit, had been sacrificed. More recent examples are numerous. In *Room at the Top,* based on John Braine's novel, veracity had to surrender to the thesis that immorality does not pay. In *Goodbye Again* the mildly interesting point of Françoise Sagan's *Aimez-Vous Brahms?* vanished when the aging lady and her boyfriend were forced into a shotgun camera marriage. But there is change: a healthier censorship climate and the bland taboos of competitive television are inevitably driving motion pictures toward sophistication.

In spite of its recurrent fearfulness, Hollywood has shown more vigor with themes that are political and social than with those that are not. American writers as a group—certainly beginning with the years of the New Deal—have demonstrated a liberal social consciousness, and the movie industry has filmed much of what they have had to say about

corruption, Okies, sharecroppers, and civil rights. On such subjects it has followed the mood and the views of the liberal segment of its audience with greater courage than in the nonpolitical relationships; it still hates to admit, for instance, that unmarried people are apt to make love. Traditionally, motion pictures have been on the side of The Little Guy, who—it so happens—is the neighborhood movie-house client. If the American press is Republican, American movies have tended to be Democratic. After all, the philosophy of the Happy Ending coincides with the American Liberal Dream.

Not many political movies have been made about the Federal machine itself. The latest one is *Advise and Consent,* the screenplay of which was written by Wendell Mayes, who "based it," as the film credits say, "on the novel by Allen Drury." But the picture is really the brain child of its producer and director, Otto Preminger. With Preminger the book is, metaphorically speaking, always in the picture. Now that he has made *Anatomy of a Murder, Exodus,* and *Advise and Consent*—with *The Cardinal* to come—it would seem that he opens the New York *Times Book Review* once a year and puts down his money for the Number One bestseller. With *Exodus* he demonstrated that an enormous, pageant-y, multilevel superstory is more convincing as a wide-screen, wide-eyed movie than as a badly written book. With *Advise and Consent* the case is more complicated.

Allen Drury's novel dealt with the controversial nomination of a Secretary of State. His nominee, and the President of the United States himself, are "appeasers" of Russia and actually cor-

Enthroned on a dolly in Washington, Otto Preminger directs Charles Laughton (far left) in his role as a Southern senator in the film Advise and Consent.

rupt men. The nominee, questioned by a Senate subcommittee on alleged dabbling in Communism, perjures himself. The President tries to have the subcommittee chairman silenced; he gets a rabble-rousing, Left-wing senator to blackmail the chairman by threatening to reveal a homosexual incident in the latter's past. The chairman kills himself, but a new senator takes over the committee—a grassroots, homespun, Taftier-than-Taft gentleman from Illinois. This man, Orrin Knox, is the real hero of Drury's book. Knox avenges the dead chairman, routs the President and his nominee, and—as a heart attack puts the President out of the way—saves the nation from the Reds.

It is a bit late in the day for a critique of Drury's book, more than 1,-600,000 copies of which have been sold during the past two years. One can only hope that the customers did not bother to take the novel as more than entertainment. The year after the novel was published a dramatic adaptation of it appeared on Broadway. The author was Loring Mandel, a television writer, but Drury—who had reserved the right of approval—was sitting at his elbow. The play follows the book faithfully. Howard Taubman of The New York *Times* called it "history turned on its head," and it is hard to disagree: Drury-Mandel's McCarthy-like senator comes

straight out of the novel as a representative of the political Left, and receives hysterical mass approval when he talks about "crawling on his knees to Moscow" (!) to avoid war; the press, *Time & Life* included, are leftists; the European ambassadors sound like the foreigners in a vaudeville sketch; and the President is not just a villain, but a villain on the level of a corrupt precinct captain. ("What can we use to threaten him?" he asks about the recalcitrant senator. ". . . There's always something.")

It is no secret that Otto Preminger, who has in his office a signed portrait of FDR looking at him, is not in Drury's political company; the answer to the riddle, "Why did he film this book then?" is brief. He did not.

He took the Senate setting, and the idea of a controversial nomination with its resulting conflicts. He bought Drury's two "buried pasts": the leftish one and the pervert one. And that was about all. A series of changes, some so subtle that it takes time and thought to become aware of them, have made Drury's indictment of Franklin Delano Roosevelt (no doubt he is the President meant by Drury, in spite of the up-to-the-minute touch added about a Russian threat radioed direct from the moon) and his "loaded condemnation of the liberal position" (to quote Taub-

man once more) into a calm and civilized movie about "the finest machine for governing yet invented," in Preminger's words, and about some people caught in a momentary grinding of the gears.

Preminger's changes were, of course, quite deliberate. During the work on the screenplay, he held up the Broadway version as an example of what he did *not* want. Preminger is a forceful man who, in a curiously uncrusading way, has fought a series of battles on tricky ground—and won them. He defied the Motion Picture Code with *The Moon Is Blue*, where the use of the word "virgin" on the sound track raised an issue of importance, even if the movie itself was silly. *The Man With the Golden Arm* broke the Code veto on the contemporary theme of drug addiction. By hiring Dalton Trumbo to do the screenplay for *Exodus*, Preminger lifted the boycott on the blacklisted screen writers. And—it is indicative of the position of strength he occupies in his world—no serious person tried to ascribe discreditable motives to this move.

With *Advise and Consent* half the battle was already won when Henry Fonda was cast as the man whom the President wants for his Secretary of State. Fonda could read the Communist Manifesto to a D.A.R. meeting and be

applauded; as soon as he appears in the committee room we know that no matter what they say, he is an honorable man. He also no longer speaks the lines of Drury's office-seeker but of a man who believes he may contribute toward keeping this world in one piece. He no longer visits and tries to sway the mind of the committee chairman (Don Murray); the exact reverse happens. We are also made to feel that the chairman kills himself not because he is hounded by a blackmailer, but rather because he is caught between love for his wife and the realization that his homosexual past is still alive, within himself. Nor is the blackmail plot instigated by the President. (This was so crude, anyway, that it is difficult to understand how Drury could have conceived of any man able to become President of the United States who is just plain stupid enough to have had a hand in it.)

Most important, in the movie Drury's hero Orrin Knox has well-nigh vanished. Edward Andrews, who plays the part, has only a few moments as an inimical senator and committee member. Good Sense is represented by Walter Pidgeon as the Senate Majority Leader, who acts more like the man he is supposed to play and less like himself than he has done in years. But Preminger's film has no real hero, and no need for one because it has no villain. George Grizzard, cast as the blackmailing senator in a very tight Madison Avenue collar, is not taken quite seriously. He does not represent any sinister forces, he is simply the *devil ex machina*. "There's only one President," Preminger said to me, "and so I can't have him a crazy man; but one crazy senator is all right." The film does not depict the U. S. Senate as a kind of Wild East with bad men (Liberals; or appeasers, if you wish) and good men (Conservatives; or reactionaries, if you choose). It shows a human theatre with people acting according to their lights; and the lights of the President and his hapless nominee actually seem to shine brighter than those of their opponents.

The point remains, how close is Preminger's Congress to Washingtonian actuality? The question is hard for any nonpolitician to answer. It has the taste of reality (certainly more so than the famous Mr. Smith going to Washington); it seemed less dreary to me than the real thing must be a lot of the time.

Preminger has filmed a political story in simple black-and-white. I am depressed only by his not sticking right to that story but feeling the need for a layer of icing, whipped up out of senators' home lives: Walter Pidgeon nursing an unconvincing affair with Gene Tierney; other, more domesticated senators feeding, lecturing to, or avoiding their badly behaved children of all ages from three to sixteen.

But I am most impressed by Mr. Preminger's ability to read Drury's novel and perceive in it the makings of a movie that will serve as its antidote.

HANS KONINGSBERGER

CHANNELS

Whatever Became of Money?

In the mail a few days ago was a somewhat curt note from a national car-rental agency which informed my wife, in no uncertain terms, that her application for a credit card had been rejected. If she insisted on renting a car, the note went on to say, there was really no way of stopping her, but it would be strictly a cash transaction, and no nonsense about it. There was also a faint implication that canaille like my wife was expected to walk from point to point, rather than to drive a car.

I found this rather heartening. It had been my assumption that in recent years credit cards have been issued automatically to anyone who was fully dressed at the time of application and had no habits that cried out for the cautious approach, like chewing betel nut. My own subteen-age son, having inadvertently scribbled his name on the back of a match folder, is now empowered to take Turkish baths ad libitum at any hour of the day or night, bills to be rendered quarterly. I myself dine regularly in restaurants where no one but the hat-check girl has ever seen more than eight dollars in cash during any fiscal year. To know that somewhere someone was refusing credit, even to my own wife, was reassuring.

This elevation of spirits vanished, however, when my wife informed me through her tears that the credit card denied her was a credit card for which she had never applied, and in fact for which she had no conceivable use. Somehow this made the whole affair that much more humiliating. To be refused credit when you ask for it is bad enough, but to have a company seek you out merely for the purpose of refusing you credit seems a little malevolent. Fortunately, it happens that I myself hold a credit card from that same car-rental agency, and I was able to strike a blow for extravagance by renting a car and taking her for a drive. She felt better after that.

I didn't. Try as I may, I cannot become accustomed to this new economy, in which money has gone out of style. I suspect I can blame my father for that. He took the view that debt, in any form, was some sort of taint, and the man who incurred debt was not to be welcomed into polite society. Anything that you couldn't buy for cash you couldn't afford. This was not merely parental counsel: he lived that way, and since he never had much cash, he never bought much of anything. But if he had wanted to buy the Empire State Building, for example, my father would have put aside the money, penny by penny, until he had $65,000,000—then he would have stepped up, laid it on the line, and demanded a receipt. The fact that the Empire State Building had not yet been constructed during my father's lifetime does not impair the validity of this story—he felt the same way about the Flatiron Building, and consequently never got to own it. Nowadays anyone who wants to buy the Flatiron Building just produces a Diners' Club card and has it wrapped for delivery.

Now that I come to think of it, this attitude was not peculiar to my father. In those days there was a breed of man called the credit manager, born with a total hostility to all their fellows and capable, as credit managers, of indulging it to the utmost. Their purpose in life was to prevent the issuance of credit. To open an account in a department store required investigation in depth of your entire life, in which your neighbors were canvassed for scurrilous stories and your picture was circulated to sheriffs in adjacent counties. Even

after an account was opened, as it occasionally was, salesmen tended to look upon you with suspicion, pushed shoddy on you, and accompanied every purchase with long, secret conversations with the executive staff.

Today, much the same takes place if you try to pay cash. Produce a large bank note some day in a department store and see what happens. Salesgirls go into a state of shock, making wild unco-ordinated gestures over their sales books. Ultimately the money is sent away somewhere to be examined, X-rayed, have its serial number checked with the FBI, and generally be handed around. Purchases that can be consummated in three minutes with a credit card—and in no time at all if you proceed on pure bravado—consume half a day when paid in cash. And the entire exchange takes place in an atmosphere of sullen distrust. Mort Sahl used to tell a story about a trio of bank robbers who steal $6,500 in pennies and laboriously haul the sacks over to an automobile agency, where they try to buy a Cadillac with them. "The salesman became suspicious right away," Sahl reported, "because he knew that *nobody* ever pays cash for a Cadillac."

I fear that I may be a little obscure to my younger readers, so let me try to say what money was. It consisted of rectangular pieces of dirty green paper that came in various denominations and could be exchanged for goods and services, like a credit card. The difference was that money was good anywhere. You didn't need different kinds of money for different shops. And when you bought something for money, you were through: you didn't have to make out checks later.

The only place where the old reverence for money lingers is in banks. It is well known that you can cash a personal check anywhere in the country, with no trouble at all, except in the bank where you have an account. If you happen to go to the exact branch where you make your deposits, it is barely possible to cash a check if you can find a vice-president to initial it. If you go

to a different branch, you will be thrown out into the street. This isn't as bad as it sounds: once you are on the street any passer-by will cash the check.

You don't even need cash to telephone from a pay station any more. This is the most astonishingly lax credit procedure ever devised. You do have to have a dime, to make contact with the operator, but after that all you must do is mutter a few numbers and you not only get San Francisco but your dime comes back. There is supposed to be a code, to keep out the ribbon clerks, but it is scarcely a secret code, and any friend who owns a credit card can let you in on it. It is true that somebody gets billed for the call, but it is never you. I am not recommending this; simply pointing out that it can be done.

It doesn't help not to like this new wild credit. I once owned a hotel credit card, as a matter of convenience, so that I could buy myself bed and board in strange cities without the need to travel with large quantities of money. (See above.) Slowly that simple, unassuming credit card has been converted into a license to steal. It is now good in 40,000 retail establishments, automobile agencies, psychiatric clinics, and saloons. It is accepted with respect and even affection everywhere except in the hotel that issued it, which now seems to regard it with deep suspicion every time I proffer it. Also, if I lose it or if it is stolen, the finder or thief can use it far more freely than I would, and I am supposed to pay for his buying spree. In short, it is far more dangerous to carry that credit card than to carry large sums of money, since any money I lose runs out, sooner or later, but a credit card does not.

I suppose I shouldn't be so querulous about all this. But I liked money. There was something special about it. What fun would it be, for example, to light a cigar with a credit card? It would just spoil the cigar. Anyway, now that I think of it, we are mad at Fidel Castro and pretty soon we won't be able to get cigars, either. The whole world's going to Hell. STEPHEN WHITE

THE SIGHT THAT MUSIC MAKES

Robert Osborn

draws an album of composers—

as he sees them

In the eight-page portfolio that follows, Robert Osborn has set himself the task of converting composers and their works—and, for good measure, a few musical performers and listeners—into cartoons. The conception is notably Osborn-like, and the execution will delight close students of his bold, unclassifiable technique (see his collection "Osborn's Americans" in HORIZON for September, 1960). Under his hand, Aaron Copland becomes a bolt of blue light surmounted by a pince-nez; Edward MacDowell, alpine-hatted and mustachioed, peers through a tangle of woodsy overgrowth; a plume surmounts the big, booming bell-like helmet of Sibelius. Whether these are, properly speaking, cartoons or something else again is a question Osborn himself might be hard put to answer. For his idea here is that of the visual impression made by music, which is not only a "serious" idea, but one with a literary lineage as well.

Sounds have texture, smells have color, sights have their sharp flavors: this the late romantic writers often declared, remarking that each of the five senses reverberates against the others, mixing and matching, so that with at least some reason—discounting for critics' jargon—one can speak of an artist orchestrating his pigments, or of a composer choosing his palette. "I invented the color of vowels!" declaimed the poet Rimbaud. "*A* black, *E* white, *I* red, *O* blue, *U* green." And earlier the introverted, pleasure-seeking Baudelaire had made a poem of the "correspondance" of all sensation. Like voices echoing from beyond, Baudelaire wrote,

Vaste comme la nuit et comme la clarté,
Les parfums, les couleurs et les sons se répondent.

Osborn, of course, has never been one to observe too closely the distinction between cartooning and pure painting. His work ranges from out-and-out caricature through the grotesque into a realm where the line between humor and the macabre has long since been lost track of. In this he is ideally equipped to see sight in sound: the bright Brazilian reds and greens in Villa-Lobos, the dramatic pattern of blacks and grays in Beethoven. His tastes in music are catholic, his verdicts on it very much his own. Even to compositions accounted as profound he brings a flick of irreverence, and even to the frivolous he bends the attention of a listener who is first and last an artist.

GILBERT _AND_ SULLIVAN

W. C. HANDY

THE PERFECT WAGNERIAN

FATS WALLER

AARON COPLAND

FELIX MENDELSSOHN

EDWARD MacDOWELL

Osborn

HEITOR VILLA-LOBOS

LUDWIG VAN BEETHOVEN

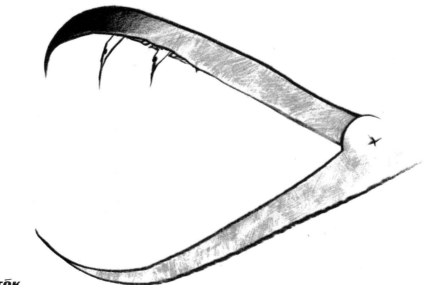

BÉLA BARTÓK

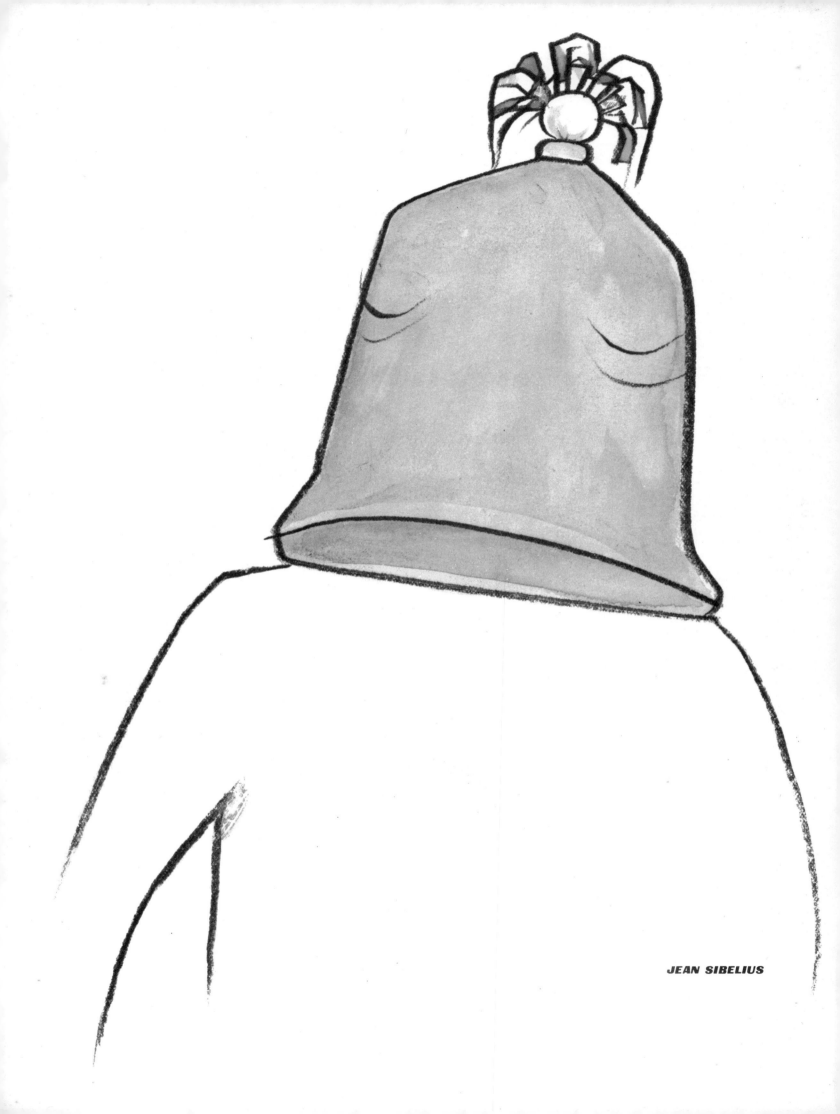

JEAN SIBELIUS